GINGERBREAD
FOR ALL SEASONS

GINGERBREAD FOR ALL SEASONS

by Teresa Layman

Photographs by Randy O'Rourke

ABRADALE PRESS

HARRY N. ABRAMS, INC., PUBLISHERS

For Kenny and Karen

THE GINGERBREAD HOUSE

Roll the dough, cut it too.
I'll make a gingerbread house for you.
In the oven, let it bake,
It takes so long, for heaven's sake!
It smells so good, pass the cream!
No! Don't eat the house of my dream.
Pipe the icing, let it dry.
The house is standing—I don't know why.
Shingle the roof, shutters on sides,
The house takes shape, I glow with pride,
Making gardens, gates, and trees.
That's my fence—don't eat it, please!
Moving at a harried pace,
Candies flying everyplace
Keep on going—just can't rest,
Get it done, here come the guests.
"Oh, it's beautiful!"—so they say
I turn and look the other way . . .
Chomp!

Editor: Ellen Rosefsky Cohen
Art Director: Dirk Luykx
Designer: Amanda Wilson

Library of Congress has catalogued the Abrams edition as follows:
Layman, Teresa. Gingerbread for all seasons / by Teresa Layman ;
photographs by Randy O'Rourke.
p. cm.
1. Gingerbread. 2. Handicraft. I. Title.
TX771.L383 1997
641.8'653—dc21   97–5132

Abradale ISBN 0–8109–8238–2

Printed and bound in China

10 9 8 7 6 5 4 3 2 1

Abradale Press
Harry N. Abrams Inc.
100 Fifth Avenue
New York, N.Y. 10011
www.abramsbooks.com

Abrams is a subsidiary of
LA MARTINIÈRE
GROUPE

CONTENTS

INTRODUCTION

Looking at a gingerbread house will make you smile. Building one will make you glow. To know that you can fashion something so whimsical and delightful out of some flour, sugar, and candies gives a great sense of accomplishment. The first one will be the most difficult—as with any first-time project—because you will wonder if you are doing it right. Take heart—if it holds together and you're still smiling, then you did it right! Each time you make another, your confidence will grow as well as your skill. Soon you will be building your own dream house.

The projects in this book should not be considered hard to make, although some do take more time and patience than others. The runners on Santa's sleigh take about 45 minutes each to cut out, but they're worth it! As with any hobby, using the proper tools makes the job a lot easier. You probably already have most of what you need in your kitchen, but the source list in the back of this book will help you find any items you may still need to find.

I have made hundreds of gingerbread houses and have received many suggestions and compliments, but one day when I was working on Geppetto's Toy Shop for a class, my two-year-old daughter scrambled onto my lap and said sweetly and earnestly, "Oh, Mommy, it's beautiful!" That was the most sincere compliment I have ever had. It is a year later, and now she wants to help. There are many ways you can let children participate, even if you are not willing to give them complete rein. Let them help you shake coconut and color to make grass, squeeze gum paste in a plastic bag to blend the color, spread icing, place shingles, roll dough, or simply squash and poke a ball of dough or candy clay. You will be amazed at how wonderful a child's imagination grows. Show them how to use an icing bag (with a rubber band to close the top)

and how to use Tootsie Rolls® like play dough. They will make marvelous buildings—usually covered with so much candy the roof will groan under the load!

By trial and error, I have discovered many ways to achieve a decorating style that pleases me. I also have found that sharing techniques with other gingerbread enthusiasts is a great source of inspiration. My hope is that this book will spark your imagination and inspire you to create something wonderful and to share what you learn and discover with others. Use the patterns and ideas in this book to make creations of your own, adding the details as you like.

In the Northeast, gingerbread houses made in November or December will last about four to six months or until the first really humid stretch of weather arrives. Humidity will destroy a gingerbread house in a matter of hours. My recommendation is to enjoy your house for as long as it lasts rather than to try to store it from year to year. Simply make another one next year—who knows, maybe even one more wonderful than the last! Start a tradition and take lots of pictures. Pictures of this year's house make great Christmas cards next year.

If you feel you must at least attempt to save this year's house, set a box in a large plastic bag. Set the house into the box (don't let anything touch the house). Put in a couple of bags of silica gel and close the bag tightly. Store the box in the hall closet—not an attic, as it gets very hot in the summer, or a basement, as it tends to be damp.

Lastly, never spray a gingerbread creation with any kind of fixative spray. Not only are the sprays toxic but, though you may know the gingerbread is inedible, a child may think it looks quite tasty and sample it without your knowledge.

GINGERBREAD SUPPLY LIST
Tools and Materials

PATTERN MAKING
patterns (given for each building)

manila file folders or oak tag

clear contact paper (optional)

pencil

clear plastic ruler

scissors

X-acto® knife

BOARD PREPARATION
½–¾" plywood board
  (for size, refer to specific house instructions)

paper to cover the board (brown, butcher, foil, or wrapping paper)

tape

drill and drill bit the size of your candy sticks

night-light assembly (see "Assembling an Electric Night-Light")

GINGERBREAD SUPPLIES
heavy-duty electric mixer

mixing bowl

measuring cups and spoons

2-quart saucepan

rolling pin

nonstick baking parchment

baking sheets

windowpane cutters (see source list)

sharp, thin-bladed knife

wire cooling rack at least the size of your baking sheets

8-point nested star cookie cutters (see source list)

evergreen tree cookie cutters

paste food color, if desired

ICING
electric mixer

mixing bowls

small bowls for mixing colors

rubber spatula

icing spatula

icing bags and couplers

decorating tips #1, #2, #4, #6 writing, #67 leaf, #14, #18 star, #47 ribbon

toothpicks

paste food colors

spoons

Candies and Decorations
ROOFS
Necco® candy wafers

Wheat Chex® cereal

Golden Grahams® cereal

sliced almonds

gray gum paste

WALKWAYS
gingerbread cobblestones

broken Necco® candy wafers (slate)

crushed chocolate jimmies

gum paste stepping stones

CHIMNEYS
gingerbread brickwork and stonework

caramels and chocolate caramels

MISCELLANEOUS
sugar sequins (flowers, holly leaves, trees, confetti)

red nonpareils

coarse sugar

green sugar crystals

green jimmies

chocolate jimmies

cocoa powder

candy canes and sticks

green jelly spearmint leaves

red gumdrops

jumbo yellow jelly candies (for lampposts)

Tootsie Rolls®

pretzel sticks and pretzel logs

sugar cones

marzipan clay

shredded coconut

royal icing

food coloring (liquid, paste, and
    powder)

brown sugar

Starburst® candies

gum balls

silver dragées

popcorn

licorice laces

Cinnamon Red Hots®

miniature jawbreakers

RECIPES

GINGERBREAD DOUGH RECIPE

6¾ cups flour

1 tablespoon cinnamon

1½ teaspoons ginger

½ teaspoon salt

1½ cups light corn syrup

1¼ cups packed light brown sugar

1 cup margarine

Cut nonstick baking parchment to fit your baking sheet. Stir together the dry ingredients in a large bowl. Combine light corn syrup, brown sugar, and margarine in a 2-quart saucepan. Stir constantly over medium heat until margarine is melted. Pour the syrup mixture into the flour mixture. Stir well, using your hands to mix as the dough becomes stiff. If you are using a heavy-duty Kitchen Aid® mixer, the mixer can handle this dough; light-weight mixers cannot. Chill the dough 1 hour or until it is about room temperature.

Preheat oven to 350 degrees Fahrenheit (F). Roll out the dough on nonstick baking parchment to a thickness of ⅛". Using the patterns of your choice, cut out the necessary pieces. Bake 12 to 15 minutes or until golden brown. Smaller pieces should be baked separately from larger ones, as baking times will vary depending on size. Check for air bubbles during baking and poke them with a knife or skewer. When baking is done, slide the parchment with the hot gingerbread onto a cooling rack. Make sure all the pieces lie flat.

COLORED DOUGH

If you plan to color a whole recipe of dough one color, stir the color into the syrup mixture before adding it to the flour mixture. If you plan to color only part of the batch, you will have to knead the color in by hand, either in a plastic freezer bag or with surgical gloves, as it is a messy job.

ROYAL ICING

1 pound confectioners' sugar

3 egg whites, at room temperature
    (use large size, not jumbo size
    eggs)

⅛ teaspoon cream of tartar

Sift the confectioners' sugar. Place the egg whites in a mixer bowl. Add sugar and cream of tartar to egg whites while stirring. When all the sugar is incorporated, turn mixer to high and beat mixture until thick and very white. The icing should hold a stiff peak. The process takes about 5 to 7 minutes, longer if using a hand-held mixer. Cover the icing tightly with plastic wrap, as it dries very quickly. Use paste food colors to tint the icing. A tiny dot on a toothpick to a quarter cup of icing will make a nice pastel color—but be sure to add it a little at a time. With practice you will learn how much to use to get the color intensity you want.

GREEN POPCORN BALLS FOR TREES

17 cups of popped popcorn (about
    ⅔ cup unpopped)

2 cups sugar

⅔ cup water

⅔ cup light corn syrup

2 teaspoons salt

½ cup butter

2 teaspoons vanilla

⅛ teaspoon green paste food color

Measure popcorn into a very large bowl. In a 5-quart pot, mix sugar, water, light corn syrup, salt, and butter. Bring mixture to a boil over medium heat. Mixture will boil up quite high in pan. Cook to 250 degrees F (hard ball stage). Remove from heat. Stir in vanilla and green paste color. Pour hot candy mixture in a thin stream over popcorn, stirring constantly to mix well. With buttered hands, shape mixture into balls. Mixture will be HOT, so handle with care. Makes about 10 popcorn balls.

MARZIPAN CLAY

8 ounces almond paste

½ cup marshmallow Fluff®

1 tablespoon light corn syrup

1 teaspoon almond extract

1½ cups confectioners' sugar

Mix almond paste, marshmallow Fluff, light corn syrup, and almond extract in a mixing bowl. Knead in confectioners' sugar a little at a time to form a smooth clay not sticky to the touch. Color accordingly and use corn syrup sparingly to join pieces. Store in airtight container.

WHITE CHOCOLATE CLAY
14 ounces white chocolate candy melts
⅓ cup light corn syrup

Melt the candy melts according to package directions. Add light corn syrup and stir. Mixture will get very stiff and have a liquid residue. Knead the clay until smooth, then let it rest on wax paper to dry. Wrap in an airtight container and keep at room temperature overnight before using. Do not pour liquid down the drain as it is a waxy residue and will harden as it cools. Candy clay will be very hard when you first use it. Knead a small portion at a time until workable. To color the clay, add a small amount of paste color to a portion of clay and knead until the color is evenly dispersed. When rolling out white chocolate clay, sprinkle cornstarch over the work surface to keep clay from sticking. If the clay becomes too soft as you work with it, set aside or refrigerate it briefly. Store candy clay in an airtight container at room temperature. Keep in mind that candy clay is a chocolate-based clay and the figurines you make from it will melt if left near any heat source—including a sunny window.

GENERAL INSTRUCTIONS

Decide on the creation you wish to make, then read through the instructions for the project you have chosen, and make your shopping list. Keep in mind that some items may only be available to you through mail order. Also, some items are only available in alternate years, so you may want to stock up on such items when you see them. Seasonal candies such as Valentine and Halloween goodies that appeal to you can usually be purchased in season, packed in airtight containers, and saved until you are ready to use them. Once you have collected all the ingredients, candies, and tools you need, you are ready to start.

1. *All the patterns in this book are actual size.* Transfer patterns to legal-size manila file folders or oak tag. You can do this by measuring and drawing or by photocopying the pattern pieces you need and using a spray adhesive to stick them to the file folders. Another option is to photocopy the pattern pieces and then cover both sides of the paper with clear contact paper. Then cut out and label all pattern pieces. Cut out all window openings with an X-acto or craft knife. For ease of marking

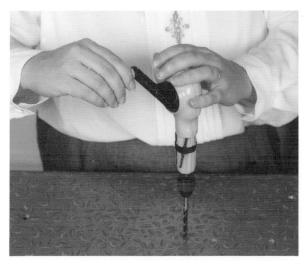

Fig. 1

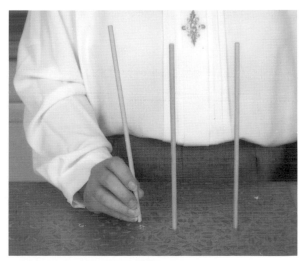

Fig. 2

details such as placement of doorknobs, hinges, and decorative icing, pierce the pattern with a straight pin wherever these occur. For decorative hinges, for example, make a series of pierces to give the effect of a dotted line.

2. Make the dough (see page 8).

3. Each building has a diagram of the layout for the "landscaping." Mark your plywood board with the location of fence posts, lampposts, flagpoles, and trees according to the diagram. Using a ½" drill bit, or a drill bit to match the diameter of the candy sticks you are using, drill holes through the board at the center point of each of these features (Fig. 1). When the time comes to place these posts, sink them into the drilled holes for stability.

4. Cover the plywood board with brown paper, butcher paper, foil paper (available in cake decorating shops), or pretty wrapping paper. Secure it with tape. Run your fingers over the surface of the paper to

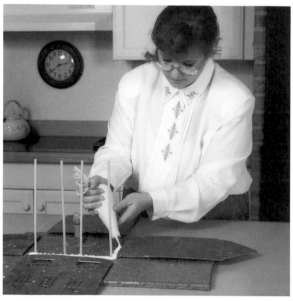

Fig. 3

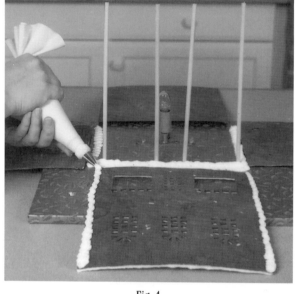

Fig. 4

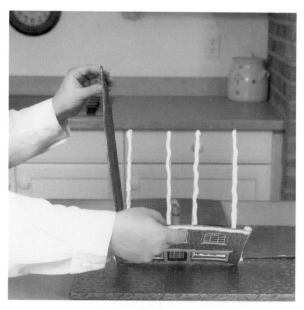

Fig. 5

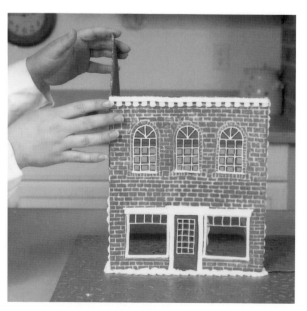

Fig. 6

locate the drilled holes. Poke a finger into each hole to break the paper. Insert any wooden support dowels (according to specific building instructions) (Fig. 2). Affix the night-light assembly to the board (see "Assembling a Night-light," page 13).

5. Roll the dough to a ⅛" thickness on nonstick baking parchment. Sprinkle a small amount of flour over the dough to keep the pattern from sticking. Using your prepared pattern pieces, cut out the necessary shapes. A very sharp thin-bladed knife or a pizza wheel works well for outside edges and a sharp knife or window-pane cutter (see source list) for cutting windows. Be sure to keep your cutting tools clean, as bits of dough sticking to the tools can cause ragged cuts. Use a pin to poke through the placement holes into the gingerbread for doorknobs, hinges, etc. Bake pans one at a time according to the recipe.

6. To cool, slide the parchment with the hot gingerbread (it is flexible at this point) onto a large wire rack, making sure all the pieces lie flat.

7. After the pieces are cool, place them in a single layer on a towel, if you have the space. Do not stack them more than two high or the bottom layer may break. Also, you can wrap each piece in paper towels (for cushioning) and stand them on edge in a box.

8. Make the royal icing (page 8).

9. Fit a pastry bag with a coupler and attach a #6 writing tip or a #18 star tip. Fill the bag with icing.

10. Decide where your house will sit on the board or use the layout diagram given. Place three adjoining walls face down on the board.

11. Pipe a wide line of icing on the board where the bottom edges of the three walls will be (Fig. 3).

12. Pipe a line of icing at the edges on the back side of the front wall where the other two walls will attach (Fig. 4).

13. Affix the walls to the base-board and to each other at the same time (Figs. 5 and 6).

14. Attach the back and other walls in the same manner. If the house you are building has more than four walls, work your way around until all the walls are standing (Figs. 7 and 8). Let set until firm (about 15 minutes).

ROOFS

Most of the roof systems for the houses in this book begin with two main pieces—the largest roof pieces. All other roof parts are added after these are in place.

1. Find the two main roof pieces for the house you are building. Pipe a wide line of icing around the upper

Fig. 7

Fig. 8

Fig. 9   Fig. 10

wall edges where the roof sections will attach.

2. Set the roof pieces on, leaving even overhangs at sides and front and matching the roof ridge edges (Fig. 9). Hold in place a minute to let icing set.

3. Pipe a line of icing at roof ridge.

4. Attach the next largest roof sections in the same manner and pipe icing at all seams.

5. Attach dormer and porch roof sections last.

6. Let the house rest so the icing has a chance to set. Now is a good time to make fence sections, snowmen, packages, or other decorations so they can be drying while you shingle the roof.

7. For buildings with cupolas, bell towers, and such, attach the main roof sections, then build up from there.

SHINGLES

When you are ready to shingle your roof, always begin the first row at the *bottom edge* of the roof. Some shingles, such as gum shingles, need to be prepared in advance (cut each stick of gum into thirds). Other shingles come out of the package ready to use, such as cereal squares, crackers, and Necco® wafers.

1. Pipe a line of icing using a #4 writing tip ¼" from the lower edge of a roof section. Using the roofing material of your choice, attach the shingles in a straight line to make the first row.

2. For the second row, cut or break one shingle in half vertically and begin the row with this shingle. This will offset the seams. Continue the row with whole shingles (Fig. 10).

3. Alternate rows one and two until the whole roof is covered.

When you come to seams in the roof where two angles meet, cut or break the shingles to fit as best you can.

Note: If you are covering your roof with material too thick to overlap, such as pecan halves or Smarties®, simply affix them to the roof in rows.

GUM-PASTE SHINGLES

To color gum paste, put 1 cup gum paste plus ¼ teaspoon black paste color into a heavy plastic bag (freezer bags work well) and knead until color is incorporated. Roll gum paste very thin (less than ¹⁄₁₆") on nonstick parchment, using powdered sugar to keep from sticking. Use a clear plastic ruler (see source list) to cut straight shingles—first cut ¾" strips vertically, then turn parchment and cut ¾" strips again to make squares. Or, use small shaped cutters such as canapé or aspic cutters to cut flowers, circles, or diamond shapes. Make enough shingles (500 to 600) to cover roof. Let dry overnight if possible.

ASSEMBLING AN ELECTRIC NIGHT-LIGHT

At night, driving past a home with lights on always seems so inviting and warm, especially on dark winter nights. So is the effect of lighting a gingerbread house. By assembling a small night-light and attaching it to the baseboard before building, you can achieve this beautiful effect more safely than was done in the past with candles. The night-light's bulbs are only 4 watts and can be safely left on for hours. The process is simple. Follow the instructions exactly. If you are uncomfortable doing this yourself, ask someone at the electrical supply store or hardware store for help. The whole assembly takes only about 5 minutes to put together.

MATERIALS FROM A LIGHTING SUPPLY STORE

3 feet of lamp cord (zip cord)

⅛ x ½" nipple

1 candelabra keyless socket (as short as possible)

⅛" I.P. fixture bar

quick-connect plug

2 screws ⅜" long x 3/16" wide (to hold light to board)

1 4-watt night-light bulb

tools: knife or wire strippers and a flat-tipped screwdriver

INSTRUCTIONS

1. At one end of the lamp cord, separate the two strands of wire by making a small cut, then pull the two wires apart to about 3" (Fig. A).

2. Use wire strippers or a knife to strip ½" of insulation (the plastic part) off the end of each wire, leaving ½" of exposed copper wire strands. Twist these strands together clockwise on each piece (Fig. B).

3. Remove the cardboard tube from the candelabra socket.

4. Slip the wires into the nipple, then through the bottom hole in the candelabra socket, one wire out each side (Fig. C). Screw the nipple into the bottom hole in the candelabra socket.

5. Curve each end of the exposed twisted copper wire strands into a clockwise hook (Fig. C).

6. Unscrew the brass screw. Fit the wire hook over it and tighten down the screw (Fig. D). Repeat for the silver-colored screw.

7. Check the connections. Make sure the copper wire twists are touching *only* the screws and the tiny brass plate behind the screw. If they are touching any other metal part (because the wire was stripped more than ½") it will cause a short in the circuit and will not work.

8. Slip the fixture bar onto the cord from the cut-end and screw it onto the nipple. The lamp cord will come out the bottom (Fig. E).

9. Use a quick-connect plug. Remove the back cover to expose a

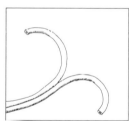

Fig. A
Separate wires.

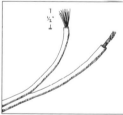

Fig. B
Strip ½" of insulation off then twist copper wire strands.

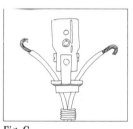

Fig. C
Slip wires through nipple, then through bottom of candelabra socket with one wire out each side.

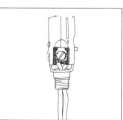

Fig. D
Make clockwise hook on each wire and hook one wire over each screw. Tighten down screws. Screw in nipple.

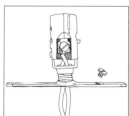

Fig. E
Slip fixture bar onto the cord from cut-end and screw it onto the nipple.

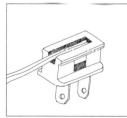

Fig. F
Lay cut end of wire into the channel in the plug. Slide the back cover on to make connection.

channel. Lay the cut end of the wire into the channel in the plug. There are two spikes in the channel; when you slide the cover back on, the spikes pierce the lamp cord to make the proper connection (Fig. F). If your plug is different, follow the package directions.

10. Replace the cardboard candelabra cover. Put the night-light bulb in and plug it in. Congratulations—it works! If it does not work, go back and try again or ask for help at an electrical supply or hardware store.

11. Attach the fixture bar to the baseboard with two ⅜" screws.

BRICKWORK

This brickwork technique works very well for **chimneys**, **walls**, and **walkways**. For a chimney, use a ball of dough about the size of a baseball. Using a toothpick, add small bits of paste food color in streaks and dots (mostly red, with a couple of dots of black) to the dough. Knead the color into the dough until it is nicely marbled. Roll the dough to ¼" thickness on parchment. Lay the pattern pieces on the dough and cut around them with a very sharp knife, leaving the extra dough in place for stability. Now score "brick" lines into the pieces about ⅛" deep. Use the back of the knife blade to make an impression in the dough. Remove the excess dough and bake the pieces. When the pieces are cool, pipe royal icing "mortar" into the scored lines using a #2 round tip. Using a dry paper towel, wipe off the excess icing and rub over the entire surface of the brickwork until the mortar is embedded in the scored lines and the bricks show through nicely. The icing dries quickly, so do one small section at a time.

STONEWORK

Follow instructions for brickwork, but instead of using red to marble the dough, use brown and black streaks of color. Then cut random stone shapes into the dough and proceed with icing "mortar."

PIPED GINGERBREAD

Place ½ cup gingerbread dough into a small mixing bowl (fresh dough works best). Add 1 tablespoon of water at a time. Stir until the dough has the consistency of stiff icing. Fill a pastry bag with this softened dough, fit with a #2 or #4 tip, and pipe the dough onto cut-out gingerbread wall sections to accentuate door and window frames or decorate the walls with scrollwork. The piped dough will bake beautifully and keep its shape.

You can also pipe the dough directly onto the baking parchment, as for the key ornaments, or even pipe out names of family and friends to attach to gifts or set as place cards on your holiday table. When doing names, make sure all the letters in a name are touching each other and underline the name for extra stability.

TREES:
LARGE EVERGREEN TREES

Make one recipe of dough and color it green. It will take about ½ to ¾ teaspoon of forest green paste color to get a deep evergreen color. Mix the color into the corn syrup mixture before adding it to the flour mixture. If you are mixing by hand, you may want to wear a pair of surgical gloves or knead it in a plastic bag, as this job is very messy. Use a set of 8-point star cookie cutters (see source list). There are six cutters per set—cut three of each size. If you place them carefully, you can fit all the pieces for one tree on a 10 x 15" cookie sheet. Using the round end of a window cutter or a small circle or star aspic cutter (see source list), cut a hole in the center of each cookie. Also cut six triangles for tree top (see pattern opposite).

Note: If you are making only half of a recipe of dough, add the amount of coloring accordingly.

Bake as directed in recipe. Assembly: Use either green or white icing for stacking the tree (white looks like snow on the branches when it peeks out). Set one of the largest cookies in place first, matching the hole in the cookie to the hole drilled in the baseboard (Fig. 11). Insert a drinking straw into the hole vertically. Using a #6 writing tip, pipe a layer of icing in and around the hole. Slip another cookie onto the straw and rest it on the icing

Fig. 11

TREE TOP TRIANGLE

layer, but twist the cookie to offset the points of the stars. Continue stacking, alternating icing and cookies, working from largest at the bottom to smallest at the top of the tree. When you reach the sixteenth cookie (or second to last) cut off the straw even with the top of the cookie (Fig. 12). Add the last two star cook-ies. Pipe icing on top of the last star and a line of icing on the vertical side of one of the treetop triangles. Place the triangles with icing so that all vertical sides are touching (Fig. 13). You can make varying tree heights by adding or leaving out cookies. When dry, these trees are very sturdy.

SMALL EVERGREEN TREES— Method 1

With a #67 leaf tip or a #18 star tip, pipe green icing onto an inverted sugar cone, icing from bottom to top in wavelike motions. Sprinkle green jimmies or sugar crystals onto the wet icing if desired. Leave the top of the cone bare so you

Fig. 12

Fig. 13

can set the tree down. Ice the top last when the tree is set in place to dry.

SMALL EVERGREEN TREES— Method 2

Use an evergreen tree cookie cutter, 3" to 4" tall. Cut three or four trees from ¼"-thick green dough. Cut off the trunk section of the tree if there is one, then cut each tree in half from tip to base vertically. Make space between pieces for baking. Bake as directed. Stand the half tree shapes in the baseboard icing with the vertical edges touching and the branches radiating outward. Add icing to vertical edges as needed to hold cookies in place.

FLOWER PLANTS

Using a #67 leaf tip and green icing, pipe three leaves radiating outward from the center. Pipe three more leaves in the same manner but in alternate spaces. Add sugar sequins for flowers.

FREE-FORM SHRUBS

Using a #67 leaf tip or a #14 star tip and green icing, pipe five to six leaves radiating outward from the center. Let set about 10 minutes. Pipe four to five more leaves on top of those with tips at alternate points. Continue in this manner until the shrub is five to six layers high, decreasing the number of leaves at each layer. Top with one leaf tip pointing up. Add berries or flowers if you wish with sugar sequins or non-

pareils. If you would like to use a base to pipe the leaves on, a spearmint leaf jelly candy works well. Let dry overnight.

SUGAR WORK

1. Tape a piece of nonstick parchment to the back of a cookie sheet along the side edges only.

2. Slip the sugar work patterns you wish to make under the parchment.

3. Fill an icing bag with royal icing.

4. Pipe the design according to the patterns with the house. It is wise to make extras in case of breakage. Set aside to dry (overnight is best).

5. When your sugar work decorations are completely dry, carefully remove them from the parchment and attach them in place with icing.

STRING WORK

String work is the little loops of icing that hang down from the edges of a roof. It is achieved by piping royal icing with a #1 or #2 tip and attaching it only at equally spaced points. Start the first loop at the left edge of a roof section (right edge if you are left-handed). Squeeze the icing bag to attach the icing to the gingerbread— keep squeezing as you bring the "string" of icing down off the gingerbread, then back up to make a loop and attach again to the gingerbread edge about ¼" from the starting point. Repeat these loops across the roof edges. Practice on the back roof

first to get the feeling of how it works and to practice spacing. Keep the icing tip very clean of excess icing, as the icing loops will want to stick to icing on the tip instead of where you want them to be. You can make them longer or shorter to suit your taste.

ICICLES

Icicles are made in similar manner to string work but are attached at only one point. Using a #2 tip and beginning at the left edge of a roof section (right edge if you are left-handed), squeeze the icing bag to attach the icing to the roof edge. Continue squeezing and pulling downward, ½" to 1", then stop squeezing but continue to pull downward to break the icing string from the tip. This process has a rhythm to it that you will discover as you practice— some icicles will be long and others short, just like Mother Nature makes them. Icicles should be made only on horizontal roof edges, as they would form naturally.

FLOOD WORK

Flood work is a technique of piping an icing outline then filling in the area with softened icing. When dry, it has a very smooth finish. Flood work can be done on parchment to make figures (prepare patterns as for sugar work) or directly onto the gingerbread.

1. Using a #1 tip, outline the area to be covered. If you are doing the snowflake cookies, outline both

outer edges and the cutout-shaped edges (hearts, squares, teardrops, etc.). Let dry about 15 minutes.

2. To fill in with the same color, use icing out of the bag and squeeze enough to cover the area onto a saucer or small bowl.

3. Adding water a drop at a time, stir the icing until it has the consistency of yogurt.

4. Using a paintbrush, apply the icing to the cookie or parchment about 1/16" deep. Do not try to paint the icing on, but rather guide the flow of it with the paintbrush. Start at one edge of the section to be covered and work your way in one direction to the opposite edge. Always work from the wet edge, or ridges can develop in the surface. The icing forms a crust very quickly, but it is still necessary to let it dry thoroughly overnight.

5. If you are using more than one color, let each one dry (about 30 minutes) before adding the next.

GARLANDS

With a #2 tip, pipe half a scallop of about 1" of icing at a time where you will place your garland. Place the green sugar sequins in the wet icing with a pair of tweezers. Complete the scallop and the rest of the garland in the same manner. Pick up red nonpareil "berries" by dipping a toothpick into wet icing and touching the tiny candies. Two or three will stick to the toothpick so you can place them into wet icing on the garland. Add

enough berries to suit your taste.

WREATHS

With a #2 tip, pipe a quarter circle of icing on the gingerbread. Place the green sugar sequins into wet icing with a pair of tweezers. Working a quarter circle at a time, complete the wreath. Add red nonpareil berries in the same manner as for garlands. Pipe a red bow or make a bow from a red gumdrop. Flatten the gumdrop with your fingers, dipping in granulated sugar to keep from sticking. Cut a bow shape from the gumdrop and apply it to the wreath with a bit of icing.

SNOWMAN

Stir together 1/4 cup of royal icing and 2 tablespoons of confectioners' sugar. Add 2 more tablespoons of confectioners' sugar and knead mixture until it is much like Play-Doh®, adding more sugar if needed. Roll one ball of dough icing about the size of a walnut. Roll two more balls in decreasing sizes. Stack the balls with a bit of royal icing between them—largest on the bottom to smallest on the top. Insert a toothpick through all three snowballs for stability. The toothpick will poke out the top. Poke a small hole in the snowman's head for his nose placement. Pipe tiny black dots for eyes and mouth. Dip a pointed toothpick about 3/8" into orange food color. Wipe off excess with a tissue. Break off this colored end and poke

it into the nose spot, pointed-end out, for a carrot nose. Pipe a colorful scarf around the snowman's neck and three buttons on his tummy. For his hat, pipe a small dollop of black icing evenly around the toothpick on top of his head. Push a black jelly candy (Crows® work well) onto the toothpick and into the black icing. The icing will squeeze out to make a hat brim. Add two holly leaf sugar sequins and three red nonpareil berries to decorate his hat.

SHOVEL

Roll out a small piece of dark gray gum paste 1/16" thick. With a pair of scissors, cut into shape of a spade or shovel. Curve the gum to resemble a shovel blade and attach a 2" pretzel stick handle with royal icing. Let dry.

PUMPKINS

1. Pipe sugar work pumpkin stems using a #1 tip and brown icing. Make extras so you can choose the best ones.

2. Color a small amount of marzipan clay orange. Roll bits of it into balls of varying sizes and shapes. Score lines into each pump-

PUMPKIN STEMS

kin from top to bottom. Poke a hole in the top of each with a toothpick. Place a sugar pumpkin stem into the hole with brown icing.

WALKWAYS:
SLATE

Draw lines on your baseboard paper to define your walkway. Between these lines, pipe about 2" of icing, covering the area completely. (Fig. 14) Set broken Necco® wafers (black, brown, and purple) into the icing in a jigsaw fashion. (Fig. 15) Continue in this manner until your walkway is complete.

STEPPING STONE

Roll out dark gray gum paste 1/16" thick and cut into stepping stone shapes, some larger than others. Mark walkway lines on your baseboard. Pipe in about 2" of icing (the icing will be green if you are using grass). Set the stones in place and immediately cover the wet icing with

grass. Continue the length of your walkway.

COBBLESTONE

Method 1: Follow the instructions for brickwork. If you are not comfortable doing the walkway free-hand, cut a pattern from a manila file folder. Once baked and "mortared," set in place with icing. Do not worry if a long stretch of cobblestone breaks; simply apply it in pieces. Lots of sidewalks have cracks.

Method 2: Roll out brick-colored dough 1/8" thick. Using a clear plastic ruler, cut 1/4" x 1/2" cobblestones. Bake 8 to 10 minutes. Cool and apply to walkway or driveway with white icing mortar.

SHOVELED WALKWAY

Frost the baseboard to a depth of 1/4". To "shovel" the walk, push the icing to each side with an icing spatula. If the mounds on the side look

too small, add a bit more icing for height. Sprinkle crushed chocolate jimmies on the shoveled walkway. Don't forget to set the snow shovel by the door.

LANDSCAPING:
GRASS

Grass is made from green-tinted coconut. Pour one package of coconut into a large plastic bag or bowl with a lid. Drop in about twenty drops of liquid food color. Close the bag or cover the bowl and shake vigorously until the color is evenly dispersed. This is a good job for children.

RAIL FENCE

Use long, thin pretzel sticks. The ones that come in snack-sized boxes are much longer than those in bags. To make fence sections that are 4" long for fence rails, lay three pretzel sticks parallel to each other 5/8" apart. Break off three other pretzels to a length of 2½" for fence

Fig. 14

Fig. 15

posts. Pipe a dab of icing ¼" from each end and at the center of each long fence rail. Making sure the space between the fence rails is even and the icing side is up, apply fence posts to fence rails. Let dry. Make as many sections as needed for your house.

PICKET FENCE

There are two ways you can make a picket fence. Method 1: Use pretzel sticks or cut rails and pickets from gingerbread. Either way, the construction is the same. Lay two fence rails parallel to each other 1¾" apart. Pipe icing on both rails. Lay fence pickets evenly into icing ¹⁄₁₆" to ⅛" apart. Repeat for all necessary sections.

Method 2: Use the piped gingerbread technique (page 14) and pipe your picket fence sections. Bake 10 to 12 minutes.

DIRT

Using an icing spatula, cover the area with brown icing. Lightly sprinkle with unsweetened cocoa powder or chocolate wafer cookie crumbs.

SAND

As for dirt, cover the area with brown icing, then sprinkle heavily with light brown sugar.

LAMPPOST

Using a sharp knife, hollow out a hole in the base of a yellow jumbo jelly candy (these look like very large gumdrops) large enough to accommodate the diameter of a candy stick lamppost.

Pipe a bit of icing in the hollow and insert the candy stick.

Pipe four lines from top to bottom, equally spaced around the light.

Pipe a cap on the lamp and a ring of icing around the light base where the candy stick post enters the jelly candy. Set aside to dry by standing the post in a cup filled with dry rice.

TIPS FOR CUTTING CANDY STICKS AND CANES

Place the candy stick on a towel or two layers of paper towel. Use a very fine serrated knife and saw around the diameter of the stick, rolling it as you go, then break it at the line. Do not try to cut through a candy cane or stick, as it almost always breaks in a way you don't want it to.

FLAG

Use a #2 tip to pipe the flag in appropriate colors. First pipe blue, let set about 30 minutes, then pipe red stripes, let set again. Then pipe white stripes. Let dry overnight. Pipe a line or bead of icing on a 7" candy stick near the top, attach the flag to the wet icing—elevate the flag slightly during drying so it meets the center of the candy stick's height.

BELL

To make a bell, use a candy mold. Melt ¼ cup of chocolate chips over warm (90 degrees F)—not hot—water, stirring until smooth. Fill several of the bell cups with melted chocolate. Set in refrigerator for about 7 to 10 minutes. Unmold bells. Cut a 6" piece of thin wire, and fold wire over to make a double wire. Twist the two strands together, leaving a small loop at the top. Insert the wire into the top and through one of the chocolate bells. Leave about ⅜" of wire (that includes the loop) at the top. Cut off the extra at the bottom leaving enough to fold into a small loop so the wire won't pull out. Brush the bell with gold luster dust dissolved in ¼ teaspoon orange extract.

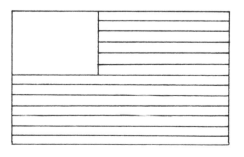

FLAG

NANTUCKET COTTAGE

1. Lay out and mark landscaping features on the plywood baseboard using diagram given. Drill ⅜" holes for tree placement.

2. Cover the board with your choice of paper according to the general instructions (page 9). Attach night-light assembly to board if desired (page 13) and prepare dough.

3. Roll the dough to a thickness of ⅛". Cut and bake the following pieces:

NANTUCKET COTTAGE

Center section front - 1

Center section left side wall - 1

Center section right side wall - 1

Center section roof - 2 (front with dormer opening, back without)

Back wall - 1

Left section front - 1

Left section left side wall - 1

Left section roof support - 1

Left section roof front and back - 2

Shed addition front and back - 2 (opposites)

Shed addition right side wall - 1

Shed addition roof - 1

Dormer front - 1

Dormer sides - 2 (opposites)

Dormer roof - 1

Bench back - 1

Bench sides - 2 (opposites)

MATERIALS

plywood board 15 x 22 x½"

paper to cover the board

tape

night-light assembly (page 13)

1 recipe gingerbread dough

½ recipe green dough

2 recipes royal icing

Wheat Chex® cereal (shingles)

7-ounce package coconut

liquid green food coloring

gum-paste stepping stones

cocoa powder

pretzel sticks and rods

lemon drop

sugar cone

green sugar crystals

paste food colors: green, brown, black, pink, violet

flower-shaped sugar sequins

small gauge florist's wire

Bench seat - 1

Note: If desired, you can use the piped gingerbread technique (page 14) and pipe door and window trims before baking. Bake as usual.

4. Roll brick-colored dough ¼" thick. Cut, score, and bake chimney pieces as follows (see Brickwork page 14):

Chimney front and back - 2

Chimney sides - 2

Chimney top - 1

5. Roll green dough ⅛" to ¼" thick. Using nested 8-point star cutters, cut and bake eight to ten of each size and ten tree-top triangles.

6. Prepare icing (page 8).

7. Make sugar work as follows, and allow to dry.

A. Tulips: Cut 30 to 40 pieces of small gauge florist's wire in various lengths from 1" to 1½". Lay them out about 1" apart on nonstick baking parchment. Using a #2 tip and green icing, pipe a line of icing to cover each wire. It helps to hold down one end of the wire as you pipe so the wire doesn't move as you work. Use a #65s tip to pipe leaves from base upward—curving some out, some in, and some straight up. Let dry. Pipe flower heads using a #2 tip. First pipe a "U" shape, then fill in the center with a straight line. Make sure the flower head covers the top end of the green icing stem. Make tulips in various colors. Let dry.

B. Make three to five free-form shrubs (page 16) or use a spearmint leaf jelly candy and pipe green icing to cover. Let dry.

C. Make 11 to 15 flower plants (page 16) in various colors.

D. Make 15 small flower plants by piping a green star with a #106 tip and setting one flower sugar sequin into the center of each. Let dry.

E. Pipe seagulls using pattern given and a #2 tip. Place a purple nonpareil for eye. Pipe gray wings. Let dry. Turn over and repipe back. Let dry.

F. **Front door lantern**: Use a lemon drop candy as a base. With black icing and a #1 or #1s tip, pipe one line down each side of the lemon drop and two lines equally spaced between them. Pipe a roundish base and top. Let dry. Pipe lantern bracket (make extras in case of breakage). Let dry. The lantern will be applied to the wall in two pieces.

8. Make a sugar cone tree according to general instructions (page 16).

9. Using black icing and a #1 or #1s tip, pipe door handles and hinges.

10. With white icing and a #2 tip, pipe window trims. Use a #47 tip to pipe front door trim. Use smooth side for top board and notched side for side boards. Use a #1 tip to pipe "Welcome" sign over front door. Let dry.

11. Prepare chimney parts with icing "mortar" according to brickwork (page 14).

12. Assemble the house according to the general instructions (page 9), beginning with the center section of the house. Then attach the left section roof support directly to the cen-

Nantucket Cottage
Layout Diagram

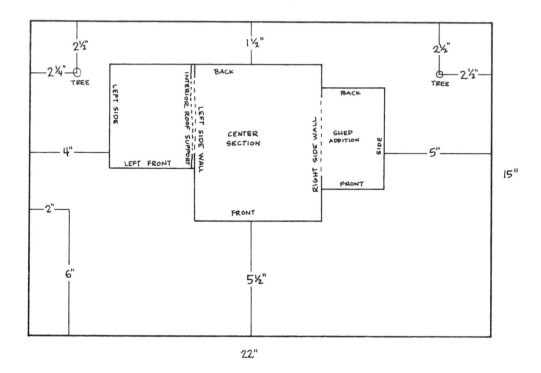

ter section left side wall, matching edges and openings (see pattern piece). After all walls are standing, let set about 15 minutes. Attach roof pieces, then dormer and chimney pieces.

13. Shingle the roof with Wheat Chex cereal according to general instructions (page 12).

14. Pipe beading over seams using a #2 tip.

15. Using green icing and a #1 tip, pipe vines on the right section walls. Add leaves with a #67s tip and small pink dot flowers with a #2 tip.

16. Attach the front door lantern to the wall with icing. Place the lantern bracket above it with black icing. Let dry.

17. Assemble the bench with icing. If you need to trim any parts to fit, either shave the edges with a sharp knife or use a very fine serrated knife to saw off the extra gingerbread. Let dry.

18. Prepare gum-paste stepping stones by cutting gray gum paste into various stone shapes (see page 18). Or use broken black, brown, and purple Necco wafers.

19. Ice the front walkway area with brown icing. Set stepping stones in place. Ice the area in front of the left section door with brown icing and sprinkle with cocoa powder.

20. Make a woodpile by cutting pretzel sticks and rods into 1" sections and stacking them, with icing to hold them together, by the left side door.

21. Ice garden areas (one at a time) with brown icing and sprinkle with cocoa powder. To "plant" flowers and shrubs, scrape small sections of the dirt away down to the paper, then pipe a small dab of green icing on the spot and plant a flower or shrub. Each tulip must be set this way. If they seem to lean, add a bit more green icing to the planting spot to hold them up.

22. Ice the rest of the board with green icing and cover with coconut grass (page 18).

23. Build stacked cookie trees over the drilled holes in the baseboard according to general instructions (page 14).

24. Place the sugar cone tree with icing.

25. Set the seagull on the roof with icing and the bench under the front window.

WELCOME

Nantucket Cottage
Center Section Front

CUT 1

Shed Addition
Front and Back

CUT 2 OPPOSITES

Left Front

CUT 1

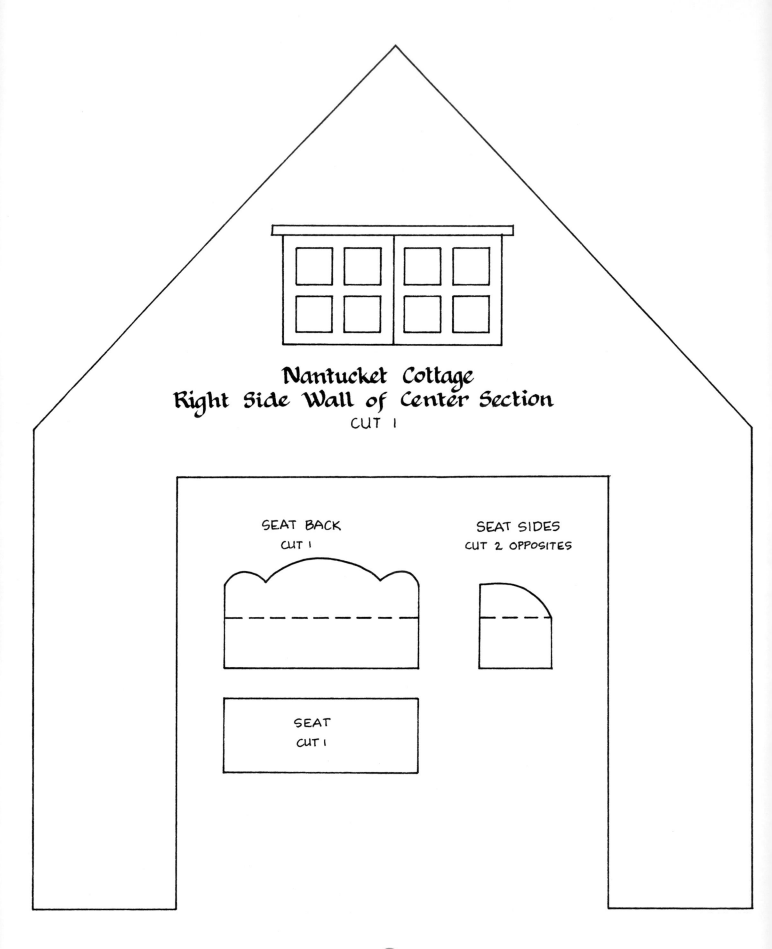

Nantucket Cottage
Right Side Wall of Center Section
CUT 1

SEAT BACK

CUT 1

SEAT SIDES

CUT 2 OPPOSITES

SEAT

CUT 1

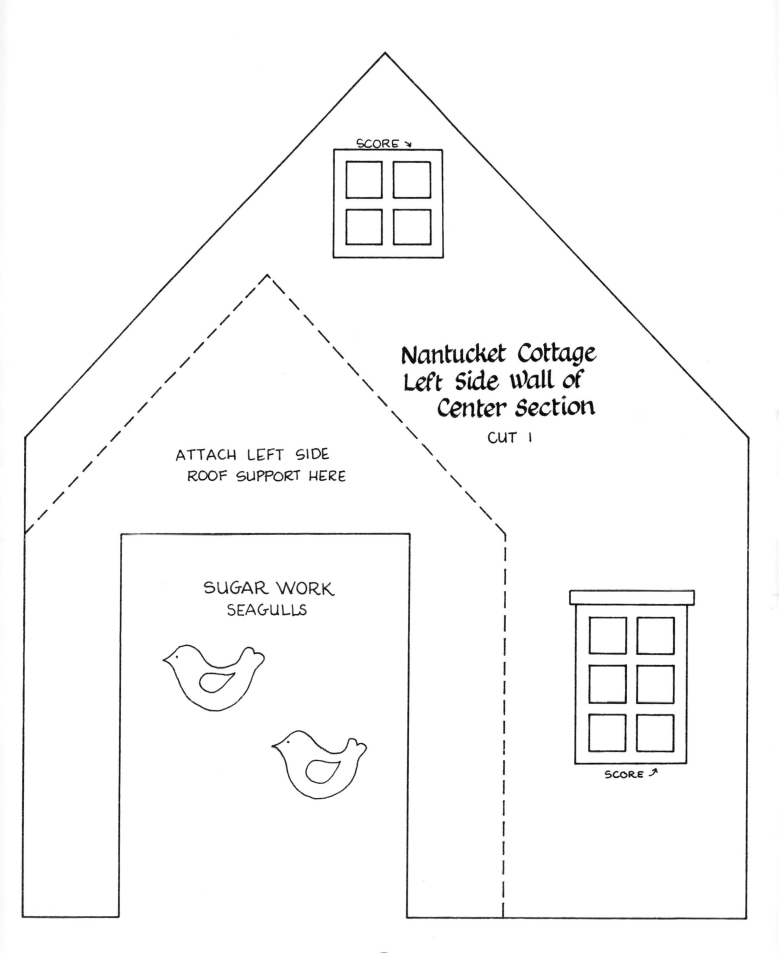

SCORE ↘

Nantucket Cottage
Left Side Wall of
Center Section

CUT 1

ATTACH LEFT SIDE
ROOF SUPPORT HERE

SUGAR WORK
SEAGULLS

SCORE ↗

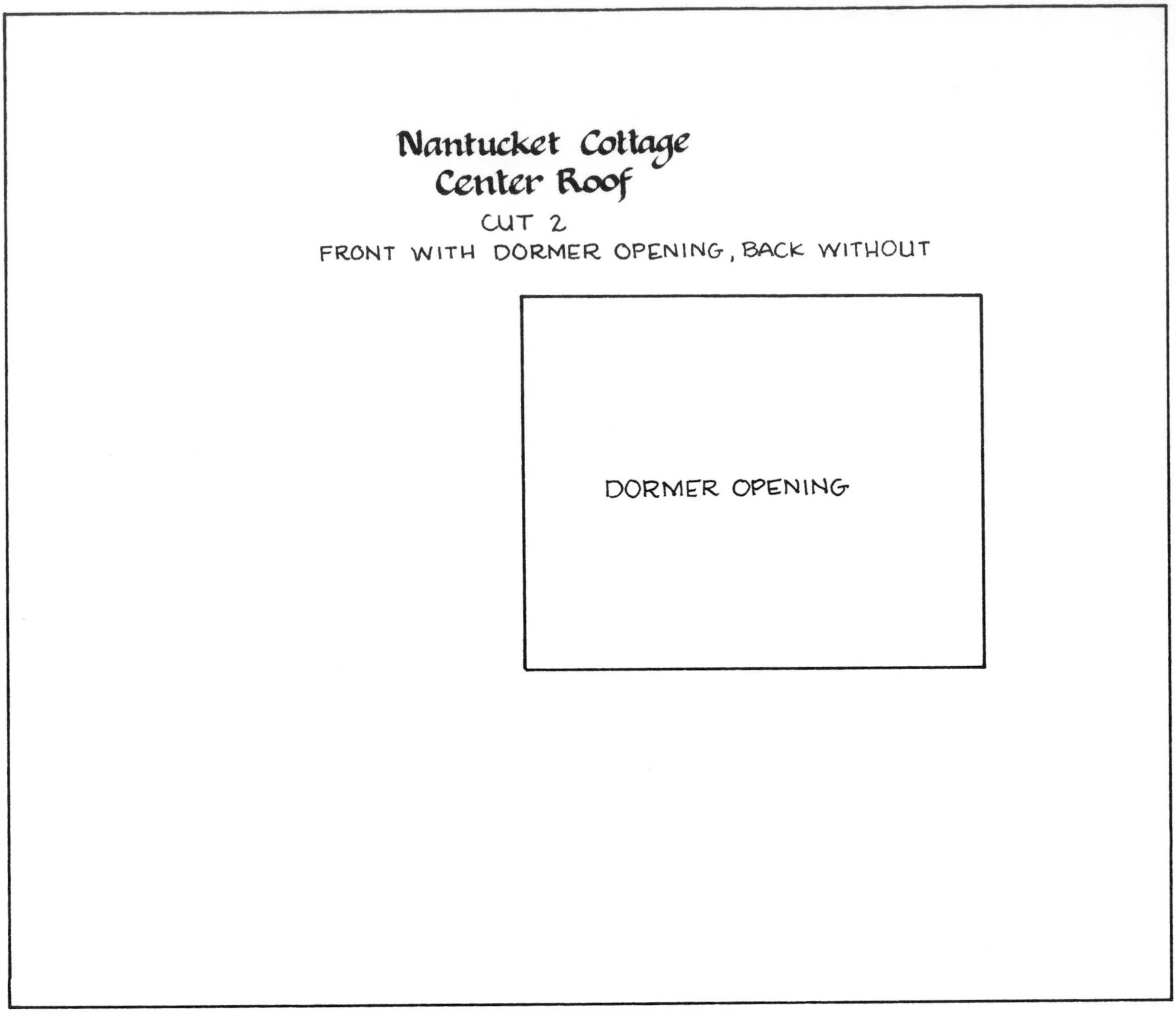

Nantucket Cottage
Center Roof

CUT 2

FRONT WITH DORMER OPENING, BACK WITHOUT

DORMER OPENING

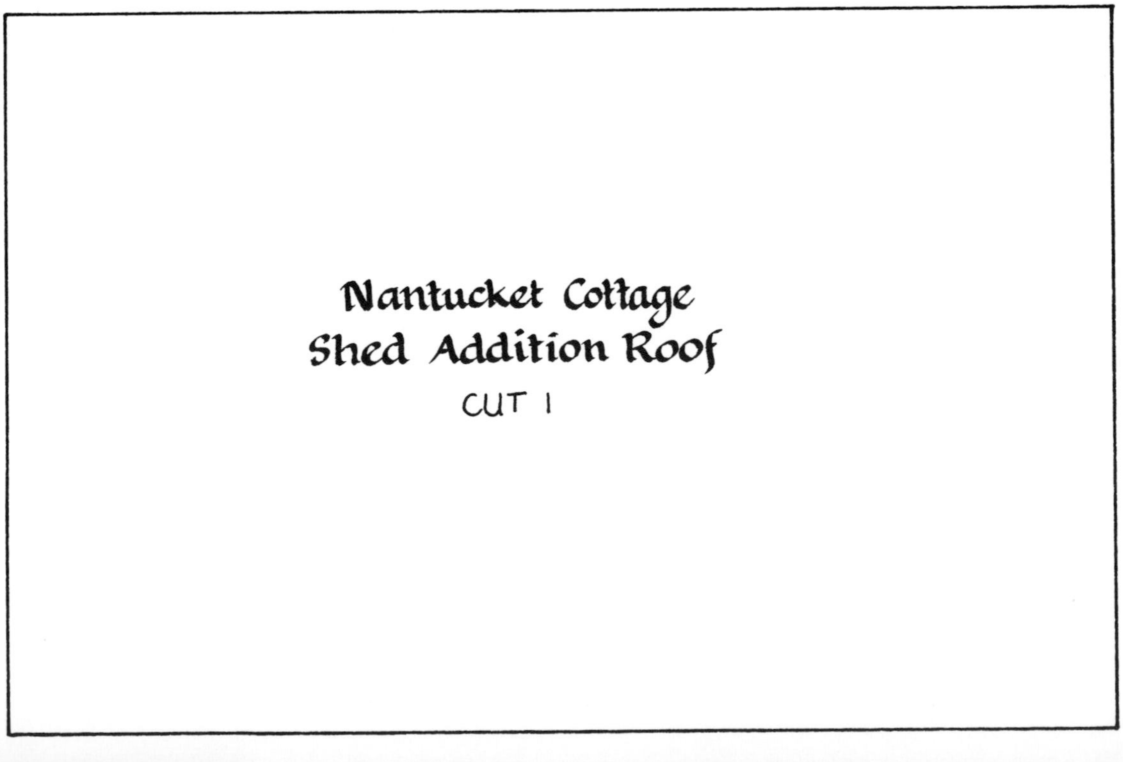

Nantucket Cottage
Shed Addition Roof

CUT 1

Nantucket Cottage

Back Wall

CUT 1

LAMP CORD
NOTCH

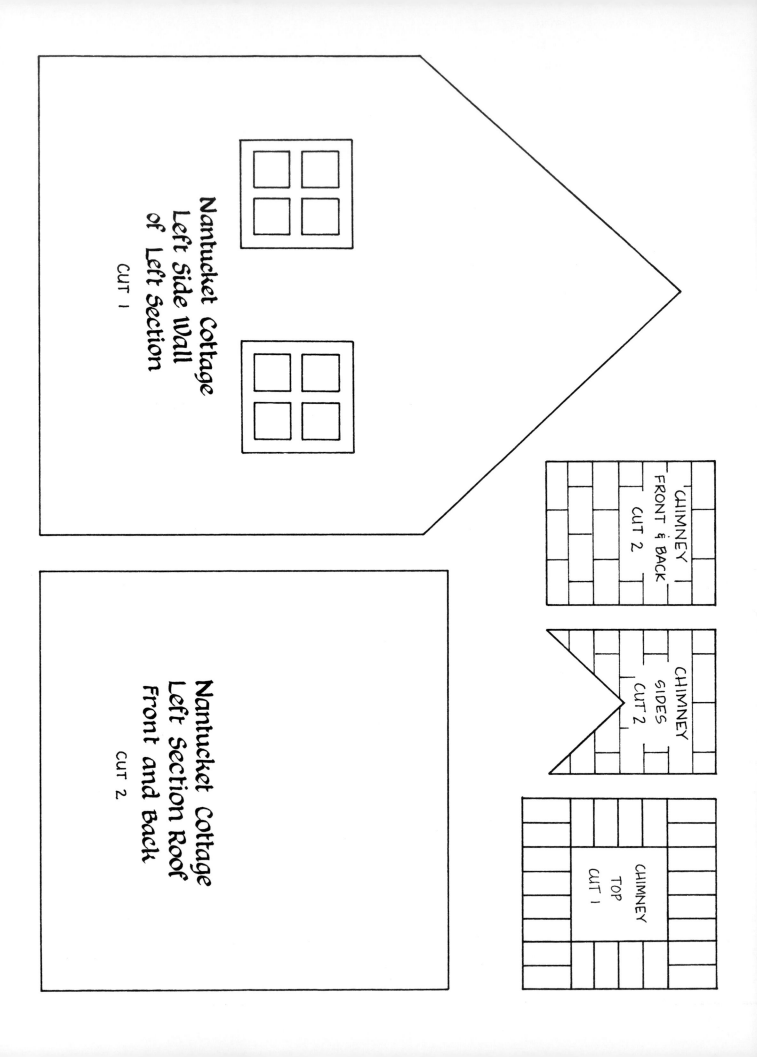

Nantucket Cottage
Left Side Wall
of Left Section

CUT 1

Nantucket Cottage
Left Section Roof
Front and Back

CUT 2

CHIMNEY
FRONT & BACK
CUT 2

CHIMNEY
SIDES
CUT 2

CHIMNEY
TOP
CUT 1

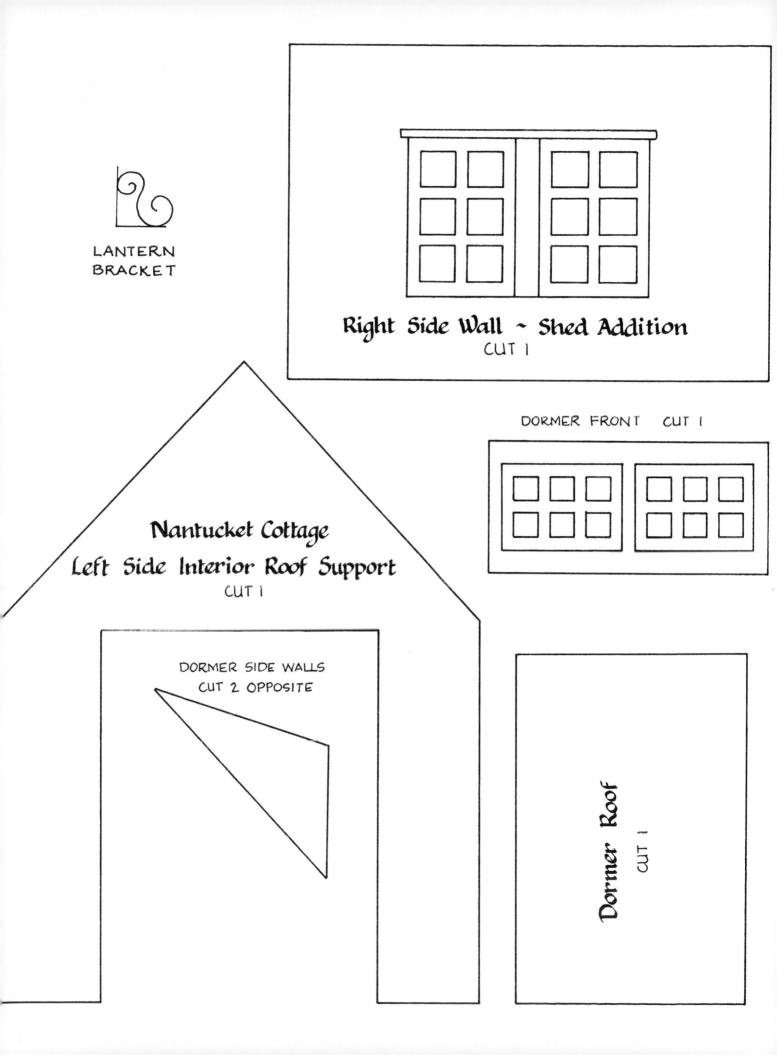

LANTERN
BRACKET

Right Side Wall ~ Shed Addition
CUT 1

DORMER FRONT   CUT 1

Nantucket Cottage
Left Side Interior Roof Support
CUT 1

DORMER SIDE WALLS
CUT 2 OPPOSITE

Dormer Roof
CUT 1

MR. MACGREGOR'S GARDEN

1. Lay out and mark landscaping features on the plywood board using the diagram provided. Drill holes for fence posts and shed roof posts using a ⅜" drill bit.

2. Cover the board with your choice of paper according to the general instructions (page 9) and prepare dough. If you would like your potting shed to be red, add the color to the dough according to general instructions (page 8).

3. Roll the dough to a ⅛" thickness. Cut and bake the following pieces, using the piped gingerbread technique on page 14 to add battens to the board and batten siding.

MR. MACGREGOR'S GARDEN

Front and back - (front with windows and door, cut back without)

Side walls - 2

Left roof - 1

Right roof - 1

Shed roof - 1

Potting bench sides - 2

Potting bench top - 1

Potting bench shelf - 1

Side bench sides - 2 (opposites)

Side bench seat - 1

4. Pipe window and door trim on front and side sections using a #2 tip

and white icing. Pipe the corner board trim and peak trim using the flat side of a #47 tip. Place the silver dragée doorknob with icing.

5. Assemble the house on the baseboard according to general instructions (page 9). Leave the shed roof off for now.

6. Assemble the potting bench with icing by attaching the sides to the shelf and adding the top (the whole assembly should be lying on its side), then let dry.

7. Attach the side bench pieces directly to the left side wall with icing to form a bench under the two windows closest to the front.

8. Make fence sections from pretzel sticks according to general instructions (page 19). You will need five 3" sections, two 4" sections, one 3½" section, and one 2½" section. Let dry.

9. Pave the area that will be under the shed roof with broken black, brown, and purple Necco wafers or the paving material of your choice, according to general instructions (page 18). Leave the post holes open.

10. Cut two candy sticks 4" long. Insert one into each shed roof post hole with icing. Attach the shed roof, with icing, to the lower edge of the right side roof. Rest the opposite edge of the shed roof on top of the candy stick posts with icing. Let dry.

11. Shingle the roof with Golden Grahams cereal squares according to general instructions (page 12).

12. Cut eight pieces of cinnamon stick 2½" long. Sink one into each fence post hole, trimming off excess as necessary.

13. Ice the garden areas with brown icing and cover with finely crushed chocolate wafer cookie crumbs.

14. Ice the grass areas with green icing and cover with green jimmies or tinted coconut (see "Grass" under general instructions, page 18).

15. Attach the fence sections to the fence posts with brown icing.

16. Tint a small amount of white chocolate clay to a terra-cotta color and shape pieces into various sizes of flower pots. Fill the tops of the pots with crushed chocolate wafer cookie crumbs. Rub the outsides of the pots with chocolate cookie crumbs to make them look used.

17. To make cabbages, tint a small amount of white chocolate clay to a yellow-green color. Break off tiny bits and flatten them between your fingers. Wrap these leaves around gum balls, layer upon layer, so each resembles a cabbage. Plant them in the garden with icing.

18. To make bean trellises, ice the tops of three pretzel sticks of equal length. Stick the tops together to make a tripod. Let dry. Using a #1 tip and green icing, run vines up and down the trellis. Let dry 30 minutes. Add green leaves with a #65s tip and beans using darker green and a #1 tip. Let dry. Gently place in the garden with icing.

19. Arbor: the arbor is made of two

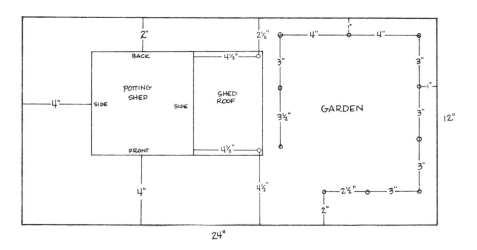

Mr. MacGregor's Garden Layout Diagram

pretzel stick ladders 4" high by 1¼" wide. Cut four 1¼" pieces of pretzel stick for rungs. Make sure they are even. Use two 4"-long pretzel sticks for sides. Lay one side piece on non-stick parchment, then glue the rungs to the side piece, evenly spaced, with brown icing. Add a dab of brown icing to the opposite end of each rung and slide the second side into place. Make two of these ladders. When they are dry, stand one at each end of the fence opening with icing. Cut three 2¾" pieces of pretzel sticks, lay each across the tops of the arbor sides, and glue in place with icing. (It may help to have an extra pair of hands for this.)

20. Make several free-form shrubs according to general instructions (page 16), adding berries or sugar sequins as desired. Let dry. Place in and around garden.

21. Make several flower plants of various sizes and shades of green fol-

lowing directions on page 16. Use different sugar sequins, nonpareils, or sprinkles to make different-looking plants. Let dry. Set each kind in the garden in rows or clusters with icing.

22. Pipe flower vines on fence using a #1 tip and green icing. Let dry 30 minutes, then add leaves with a #65s tip and little pink icing buds with a #1 tip. Let dry.

23. Make bunnies for the garden by rolling tiny pieces of white chocolate clay. First make the body, then add the head and ears, then the legs. Refrigerate if necessary to harden the clay. Pipe tiny white dots for eyes and add nonpareil pupils. Use black icing to pipe a tiny nose and mouth. Let dry. Place bunnies in garden.

24. Make a shovel according to general instructions (page 17). Place against wall under shed roof with icing.

25. For gloves, flatten a piece of white chocolate clay, cut two small mitten shapes, then cut fingers into

the mittens. Rub each with crushed cookie crumbs to make them look used and place on potting bench with icing.

26. Tall stem flowers (tulips, daisies, purple spikes): cut several pieces of small-gauge florist's wire in various lengths from 1" for tulips to 1¾" for purple spikes. Lay them out about 1" apart on nonstick parchment. Using a #2 tip and green icing, pipe a line of icing to cover each wire. It helps to hold down one end of the wire as you

pipe so the wire doesn't move as you work. Use a #65s tip to pipe leaves from the base upward, curving some out, some in, and others straight up. Let dry. Pipe tulip flowers according to directions on page 20. Pipe daisies using small dots of yellow and white and a #1 tip. Pipe purple spikes up the top part of the stem using a #1 tip and purple icing. Let dry. Carefully place the flowers around the garden and shed with icing.

Potting Shed Front and Back

CUT FRONT WITH WINDOWS, CUT BACK WITHOUT

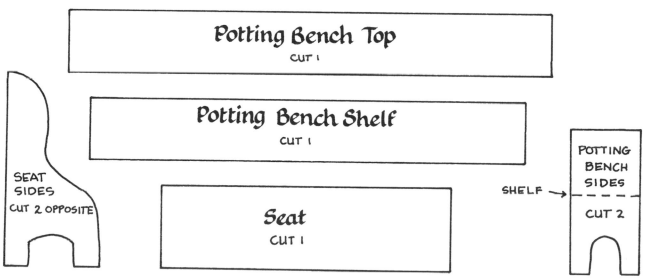

Potting Bench Top

CUT 1

Potting Bench Shelf

CUT 1

SEAT
SIDES

CUT 2 OPPOSITE

Seat

CUT 1

POTTING
BENCH
SIDES

SHELF →

CUT 2

Potting Shed
Shed Roof

CUT 1

Potting Shed
Right Side Roof

CUT 1

Potting Shed
Left Side Roof

CUT 1

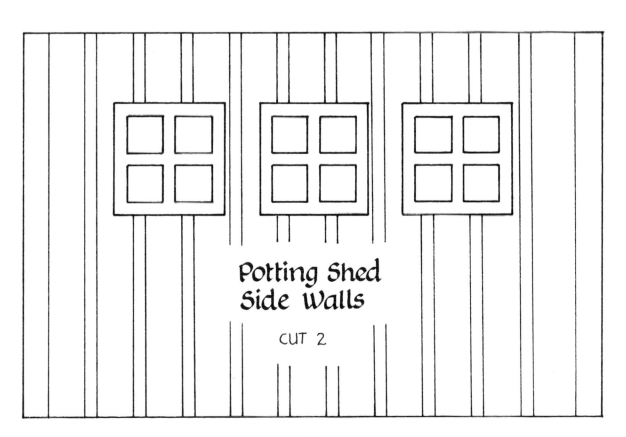

Potting Shed
Side Walls

CUT 2

BABY CARRIAGE

Prepare dough and chill as directed. Roll dough to a ⅛" thickness on nonstick baking parchment. Cut and bake the following pieces:

BABY CARRIAGE

Side - 2 (opposites)

Bottom panel - 1

Front panel - 1

Back panel - 1

Hood panel #1 - 1

Hood panel #2 - 1

Hood panel #3 - 1

Hood panel #4 - 1

Slats for curves - 9

Interior platform - 1

Interior platform supports - 2

Wheels - 4

Under-carriage supports - 2

Axle spacers - 2

1. Pipe sugar work carriage handle bar and handles using a #12 tip. Let dry. Turn over and pipe a crescent on the curl part of the handle.

2. Flood all outside surfaces and let dry overnight (see flood work page 16). Pipe "stitches" on side panels with a #1 tip.

3. Attach interior platform supports to wrong side of baby carriage sides, 1" down from flat edge (see fig. A).

4. Place bottom facedown on a towel. With a #6 tip, pipe a line of icing along both long edges. Place sides,

MATERIALS

Tray or baseboard (approximately 12" diameter)

10" doily

1 recipe gingerbread dough

2 recipes royal icing

2 candy sticks

Coral, Nu-Silver® and Silk White® luster dust

orange or lemon extract

marzipan clay (page 8)

paste food colors: forest green, pink, blue, violet

black food color pen

icing side out, perpendicular on bottom piece using soup cans to hold sides. Pipe extra icing inside along seams—sides will sit on TOP of bottom piece, not next to it.

5. Place #3 hood section with icing so it spans the distance from one side of carriage to the other side. Place #4 hood section, attaching it to sides and #3 hood section with icing.

6. Check interior platform for fit; if it needs to be narrower, shave the edges with a knife until it slips easily into place. Set on interior platform supports with icing.

7. Place #2 hood, #1 hood, front and back panels with icing. Let dry 2 hours.

8. Carefully turn over and place slats

to span side to side on curved edges. Attach slats to sides and to each other with icing. Let dry.

9. Use a #104 tip and pipe ruffles around inside edges of carriage in a wavelike motion. Let dry.

10. Fill any gaps in seams using a #4 tip. Smooth seams and then pipe #4 tip beads over slat seams and #6 tip beads over all side seams and on gingerbread edges around carriage opening (the part where the baby goes in). NOTE: Set carriage up on two cans to do hard-to-reach underneath seams.

11. To color wheels, mix equal parts of "Nu-Silver" and "Silk White" luster dust (see source list) with a few drops of orange or lemon extract. Paint onto wheels with a soft paintbrush. Let dry.

12. Ice inside bed of carriage using an icing spatula. Build up pillow area with icing from a bag and a #6 tip. Let dry.

13. Pipe frills around "pillow" using a #14 star tip. Let dry.

14. To make a baby, color about ⅓ cup marzipan clay (page 8) to the skin tone of your choice. Roll a ball of the marzipan about 1" wide by 1¼" long. Use a knife to make an indentation across the eye area. Press the blade of the knife flat against the

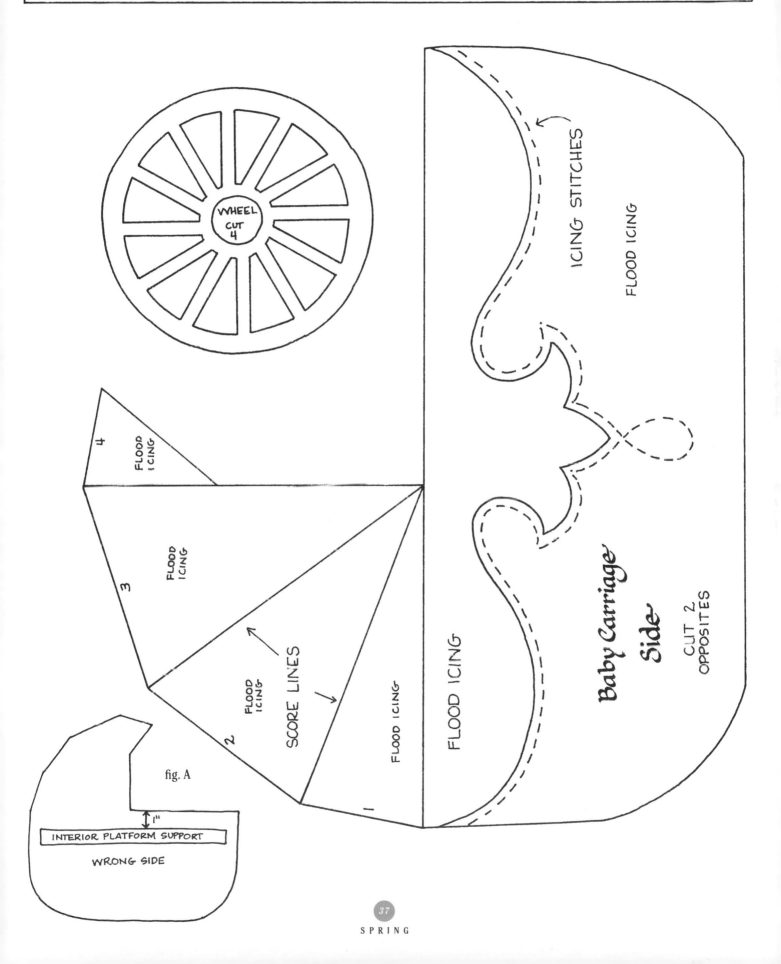

WHEEL
CUT
4

ICING STITCHES

FLOOD ICING

FLOOD ICING

4

FLOOD ICING

3

FLOOD ICING

2

FLOOD ICING

SCORE LINES

FLOOD ICING

FLOOD ICING

Baby Carriage
Side
CUT 2
OPPOSITES

fig. A

1"

INTERIOR PLATFORM SUPPORT

WRONG SIDE

forehead of the baby's face.

Roll a tiny nose and stick in place. Pipe two tiny white dots for eyes and place a light blue (or other appropriate color) piece of sugar sequin or nonpareil for the iris. Use a food color pen to make a dot pupil on each iris. Dust cheeks and nose lightly with coral luster dust.

15. Pipe white icing around baby's head for a bonnet covering the top and sides of the head; it is not necessary to do the back. Pipe a ruffle around the bonnet with a #101s tip and a bow with a #1 tip. Let dry.

16. When dry, place baby's head on pillow area with icing. Roll a marzipan body 1" wide x 2" long, and about ½" thick. Place body in carriage bed touching baby's head at the neck.

17. To make quilt, roll a piece of uncolored marzipan clay about ⅛" thick. Cut a rectangle 3 x 4". Score a simple quilt block design into the surface using the point of a sharp knife. Use very diluted food colors to paint the blocks of the quilt. With the point of a sharp knife, score a quilting design into the marzipan quilt around the borders and in the blocks if desired. Fold over the top edge of the marzipan quilt and place it over the baby's body leaving some soft folds.

18. On the base of your choice (i.e., platter, tray, or board), assemble the axle supports and axle spacers into a square. Supports go left to right, spacers go front to back, attaching them to the base and to each other at the corners. Let dry.

19. Cut two candy sticks to a length of 5¾". Check to be sure the candy sticks fit the holes in the wheels; shave off the candy stick to fit if necessary. Glue one to each axle support so that the ends extend evenly out each side. Slip one wheel onto each candy stick and ice the tip that pokes through. Let dry.

20. With a #6 tip, run icing lines along upper edges of candy stick axles. Set carriage in place on axles.

21. Attach one carriage handle arm to each side of the carriage with icing so the curls of the arms extend evenly to the front. Let dry. Set the handle into the piped crescents with icing.

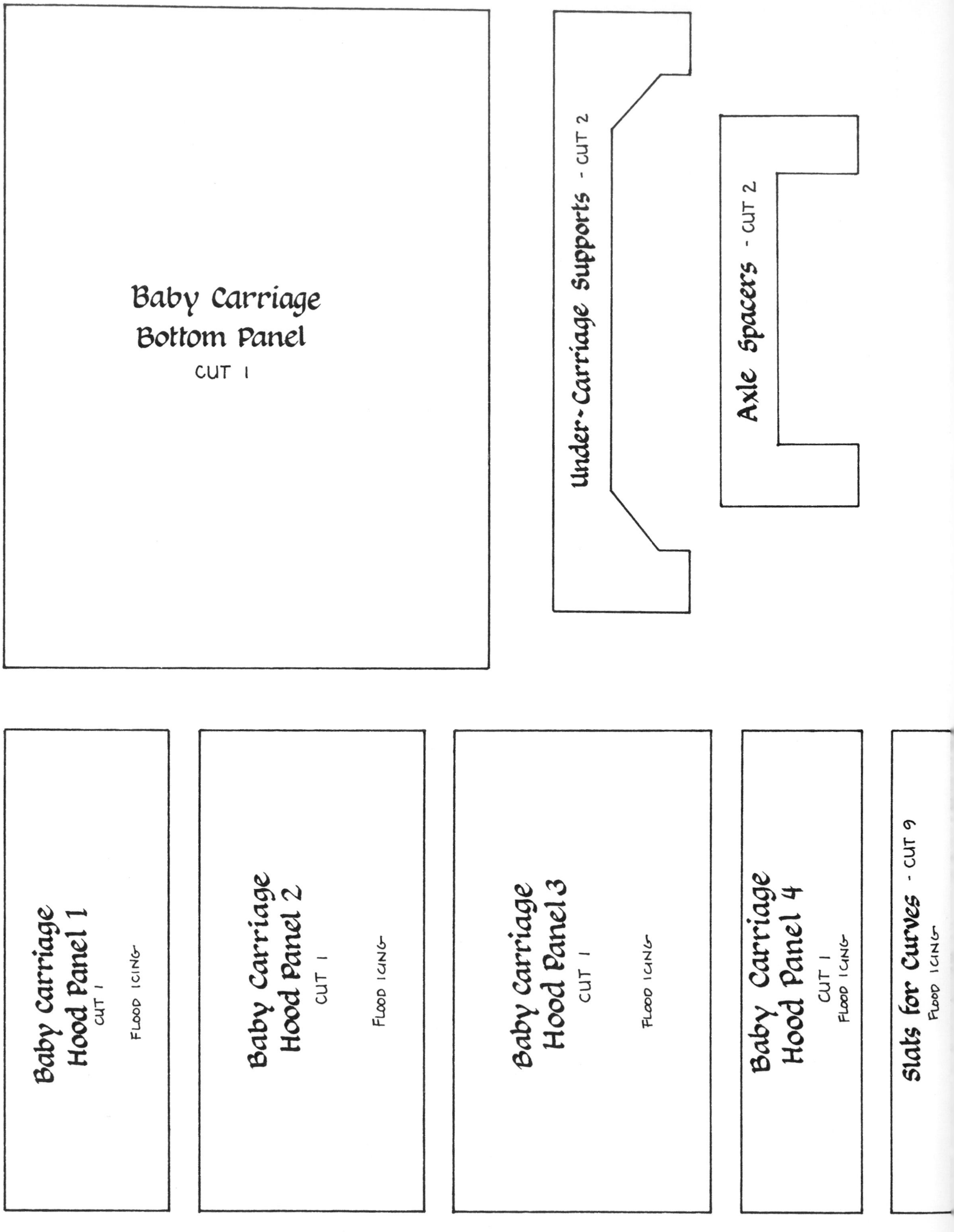

Baby Carriage
Bottom Panel
CUT 1

Under-Carriage Supports - CUT 2

Axle Spacers - CUT 2

Baby Carriage
Hood Panel 1
CUT 1
FLOOD ICING

Baby Carriage
Hood Panel 2
CUT 1
FLOOD ICING

Baby Carriage
Hood Panel 3
CUT 1
FLOOD ICING

Baby Carriage
Hood Panel 4
CUT 1
FLOOD ICING

Slats for Curves - CUT 9
FLOOD ICING

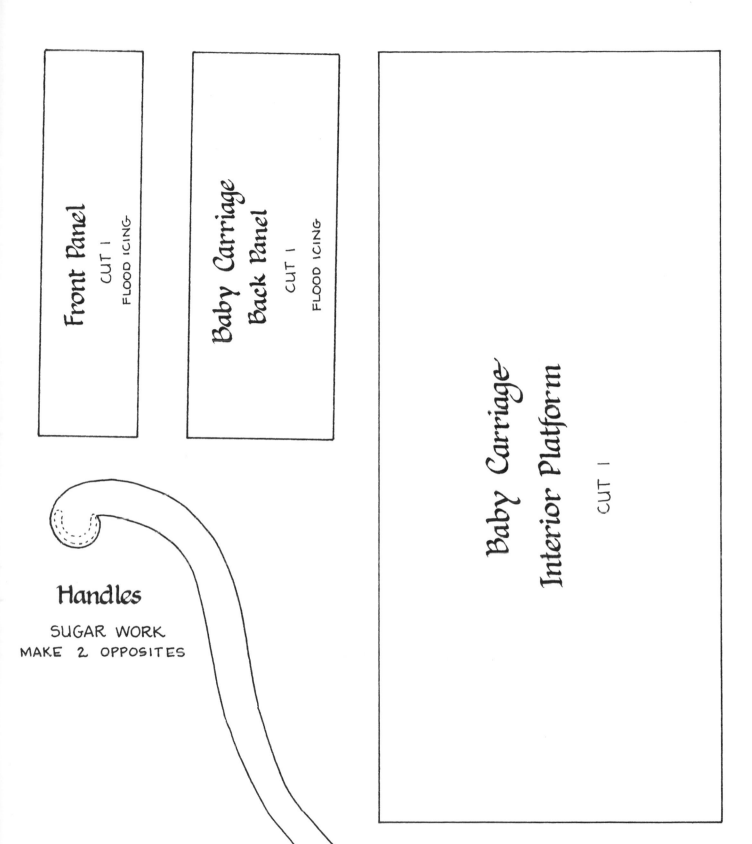

Front Panel
CUT 1
FLOOD ICING

Baby Carriage
Back Panel
CUT 1
FLOOD ICING

Baby Carriage
Interior Platform
CUT 1

Handles

SUGAR WORK
MAKE 2 OPPOSITES

SUGAR WORK HANDLEBAR - MAKE 1

LIGHTHOUSE

1. Cover the baseboard with paper and secure with tape according to general instructions (page 9).

2. Lay out house placement and landscaping features on 3"-thick Styrofoam (available in lumber yards—it has a foil covering on both sides) according to diagram.

3. For sandy cliff, cut away excess Styrofoam with a serrated knife. When cutting, it is easiest to remove 4" to 8" pieces of the styrofoam. Do not try to cut the whole section away in one piece. This only needs to be rough, as it will be covered in icing and brown sugar. Cut some sections at 90 degree angles and some at 45 to 60 degree angles. The back and the left side should be vertical. Check for fit on the baseboard, then cover the back and left side with the same paper as used on the baseboard.

4. With white glue, glue the Styrofoam to the baseboard, matching back and left side edges. Let dry.

5. Make one recipe of dough. Cut and bake the following pieces:

LIGHTHOUSE

Front - 1

Back - 1

Left side - 1

Right side - 1

Panel A - 4 (1 with windows and door, 2 with windows only, 1 plain)

Panel B - 4 (1 with bell beam hole, 3 plain)

Panel C - 4 with aspic star cut-out

Panel D - 4

Roof front - 1

Roof back - 1

Platform 1 - 1

Platform 2 - 1

Porch peak - 1

Porch peak roof - 2 (opposites)

Corbels - 8

Window box - 3 (1 front, 2 side)

6. Roll brick colored dough ¼" thick. Cut, score, and bake the following pieces:

Chimney - 1

Chimney sides - 2

Chimney front and back - 2

Chimney top - 1

125 cobblestones (¼ x ½ x ⅛" thick)

7. Roll a small piece of black dough very thin. Cut and bake the following pieces:

Lighthouse tower roof - 8

8. Following instructions for piped gingerbread (page 14), using black dough, pipe and bake the following pieces:

Lighthouse

Panel E - 8

Platform 1 railings - 8

Platform 2 railings - 8

9. Make ½ recipe green dough (page 8). Using nested 8-point star cutters, cut and bake six of each size and five tree-top triangles. Cut more if you want more than one tree.

10. Using the flood work technique

(page 16), cover the A and B panels with icing. Do the red squares first and let dry, then proceed with the white areas. Let dry completely.

11. Using a #47 ribbon tip, pipe siding onto the front, back, and side walls of the house. Let dry.

12. Pipe window frames using a #4 tip.

13. Using food coloring pens (see source list) or a paintbrush and liquid food colors, color in the sunburst on the porch peak as desired. Let dry.

14. Following directions for sugar work (page 16), make sugar work bicycle and 12 to 15 flower plants (page 16) in varying sizes.

15. Make a bell (page 19).

16. Make a sugar cone tree (page 16).

17. Make two to three free-form shrubs (page 16).

18. Pipe hinges and door knobs on doors using a #1 tip and black icing.

19. Mortar chimney pieces according to general instructions (page 14).

20. To get a footprint of the lighthouse on the Styrofoam, tape the pattern pieces together and set them where you wish to build the house on the board. (See photo/diagram.) Use the Platform 1 piece to find placement of dowels for tower walls. Place a pin or nail through the pattern into the Styrofoam to mark dowel placements. Remove the pattern piece and poke the dowels into the Styrofoam as far as they will go, being careful to keep them as straight as possible.

21. If you wish to have a night-light in the house, follow instructions for assembling a night-light (page 13) but you will have to hot glue the fixture bar to the foil on the Styrofoam as screws will not hold it.

22. Using a #6 round or a #18 star tip, pipe icing onto the two dowels

MATERIALS

plywood board 24 x 24 x ½"
Styrofoam 24 x 24 x 3" (available at lumber yards)
paper to wrap the board
tape
night-light assembly (see page 13)
hot glue gun and glue stick
1 recipe gingerbread dough
½ recipe green dough
4-5 recipes royal icing
Wheat Thins® crackers (broken into quarters for shingles)
sheet gelatin
1 yellow jumbo jelly candy
1 bamboo skewer
8 wooden dowels ¼ x 17"
1 red miniature jawbreaker
1 pretzel rod 7" long
1 pretzel stick
thin wire
chocolate chips
bell candy mold
gold luster dust
orange extract
flower sugar sequins
2 candy sticks (porch posts)
sugar cone
green jimmies
paste food colors: black, red green, blue, brown
spearmint leaves jelly candies
coconut
brown sugar
candy rocks
star jelly candy
gingerbread cobblestones (about 120; see page 18)
cocoa powder

that make the diagonal wall of the house and onto the Styrofoam base. Attach a B panel to the dowels and the baseboard. Measure up 5½" and attach the bell beam support on the inside of the panel.

23. Continue adding the A and B panels according to the layout diagram, icing the dowels as you go. When you add the B panel opposite the first panel, use the one with the hole for the bell beam.

24. Use a large needle (#3 crewel) to poke a hole about ½" from the end of a 7"-long pretzel rod. Then insert the pretzel rod (bell beam) into the hole in the B panel (the end with the hole should stick out of the wall) and attach it to the support on the opposite wall with icing.

25. Continue adding the A and B panels until all are standing.

26. Glue Platform 1 to the tops of the tower walls with icing.

27. Assemble the house walls and roof as per general instructions and according to the layout diagram.

28. Attach chimney pieces with icing.

29. Glue corbels to underside of Platform 1 and tower seams with icing.

30. Make porch roof separately and let dry.

31. Attach window boxes with icing.

32. Stand up C and D panels alternately on Platform 1. Let set.

33. Glue Platform 2 in place on top of C and D panels.

34. Pipe decorative beads at seams with a #14 star tip.

35. Use scissors to cut sheet gelatin to fit E panels. Glue one piece of sheet gelatin to each E panel with black icing.

36. Cut a bamboo skewer to 2⅞" in length. Push the pointed end into the top center of a jumbo size jelly candy. Glue this to the center of Platform 2 with icing for a light.

37. Assemble the E panels using black icing around the jelly light. Let dry. Then add the black roof pieces with black icing using the top of the skewer as a center point and roof support.

38. Top with a small red ball candy.

39. Stand the Platform 1 and Platform 2 railings around the edges of their platforms with black icing. Trim to fit where necessary.

40. To hang up the bell, push the wires up through the hole in the bell beam pretzel—twist or bend loop over to secure.

41. For porch posts, push the candy sticks into the Styrofoam, just far enough so that their tops are even with the lower edge of the roof. Make sure they are straight. Attach the porch roof to the roof and the tops of the porch posts with icing.

42. Shingle the roof according to general instructions (page 12) using Wheat Thins crackers broken into smaller pieces.

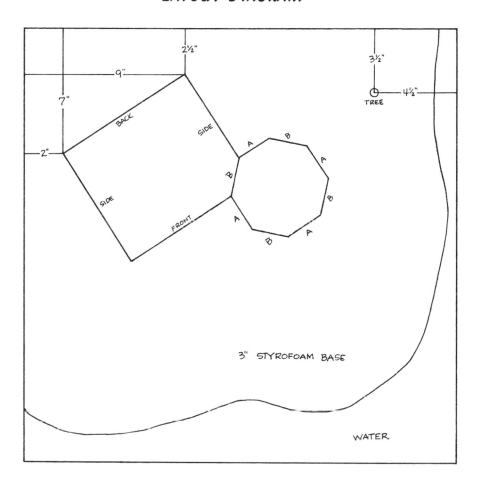

LIGHTHOUSE LAYOUT DIAGRAM

43. Pipe green icing leaves with a #65s tip in the window boxes and add sugar sequin flowers.

44. Use a #1 tip to pipe a vine up the right side porch post and across the porch peak. Then use a #65s tip for leaves. Set pink sugar sequins for flowers.

45. Pave the walkway with cobblestones (see page 18).

46. Ice the garden areas with brown icing and cover with cocoa powder or chocolate cookie crumbs, then plant your flowers, shrubs, and sugar cone tree with icing.

47. Assemble the stacked cookie tree in place according to general instructions (page 14).

48. To make sandy cliffs, ice the cut edges of the Styrofoam with light brown icing and immediately cover with brown sugar sand. You may need to reapply the sand, as the moisture in the icing absorbs the sugar. Work in 8" to 10" sections at a time.

49. Cover the grass areas according to general instructions (page 18).

50. To make waves, use white and *very* light blue icing and an icing spatula. Spread the colors, pressing the spatula into the icing to make it mingle but not mix; the pressing action will make the icing squeeze out in places to make rolling, wave-like impressions. Work your way around the cliffs in this manner.

51. Set in piles of candy rocks and maybe a star jelly candy for a starfish.

52. Set bicycle in place with icing.

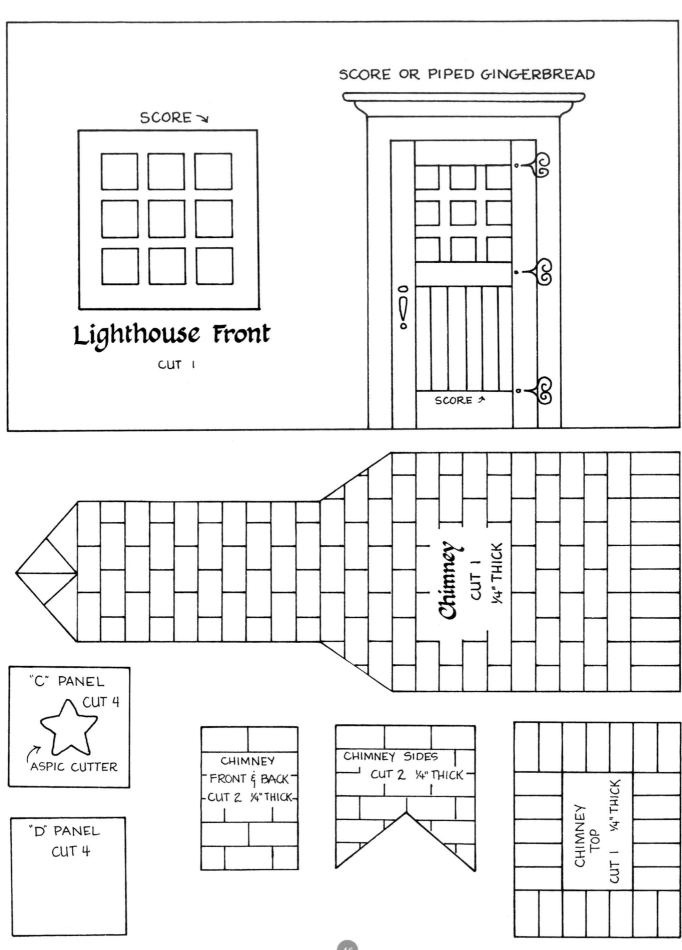

SCORE ↘

SCORE OR PIPED GINGERBREAD

Lighthouse Front

CUT 1

SCORE ↗

Chimney
CUT 1
¼" THICK

"C" PANEL
CUT 4
← ASPIC CUTTER

"D" PANEL
CUT 4

CHIMNEY
FRONT & BACK
CUT 2 ¼" THICK

CHIMNEY SIDES
CUT 2 ¼" THICK

CHIMNEY TOP
CUT 1 ¼" THICK

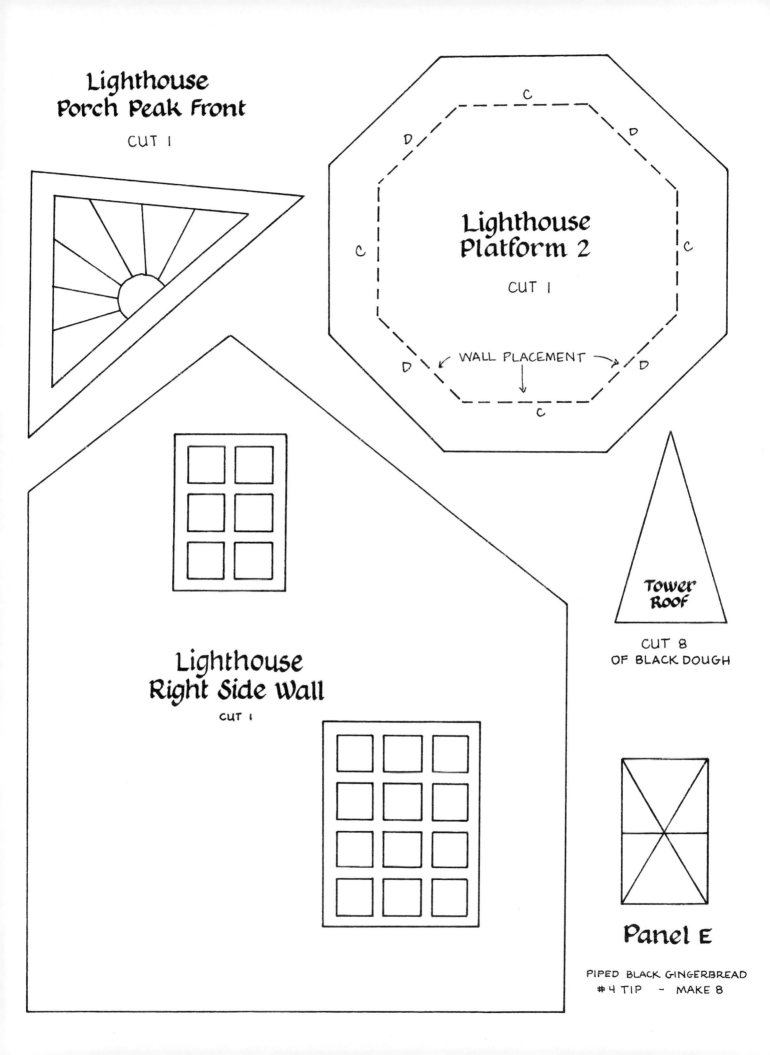

Lighthouse
Porch Peak Front
CUT 1

Lighthouse
Platform 2
CUT 1

C

D   D

C   C

D   D

← WALL PLACEMENT →

C

Lighthouse
Right Side Wall
CUT 1

Tower Roof

CUT 8
OF BLACK DOUGH

Panel E

PIPED BLACK GINGERBREAD
#4 TIP — MAKE 8

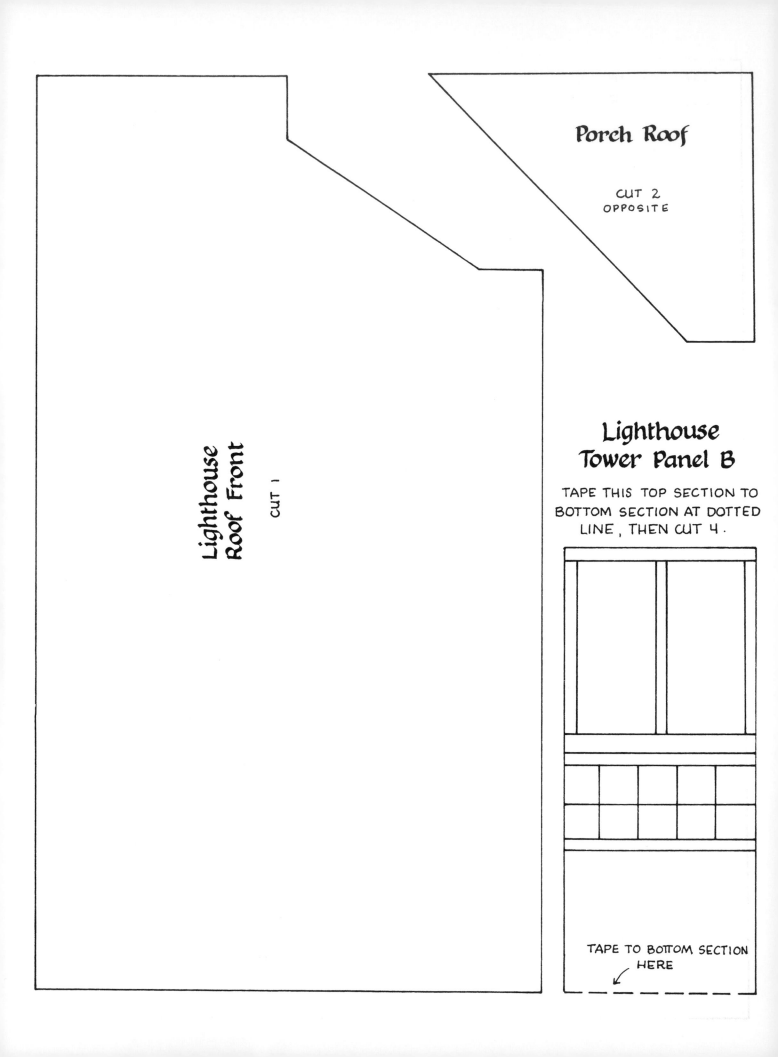

Porch Roof

CUT 2
OPPOSITE

Lighthouse
Roof Front

CUT 1

**Lighthouse
Tower Panel B**

TAPE THIS TOP SECTION TO
BOTTOM SECTION AT DOTTED
LINE, THEN CUT 4.

TAPE TO BOTTOM SECTION
HERE

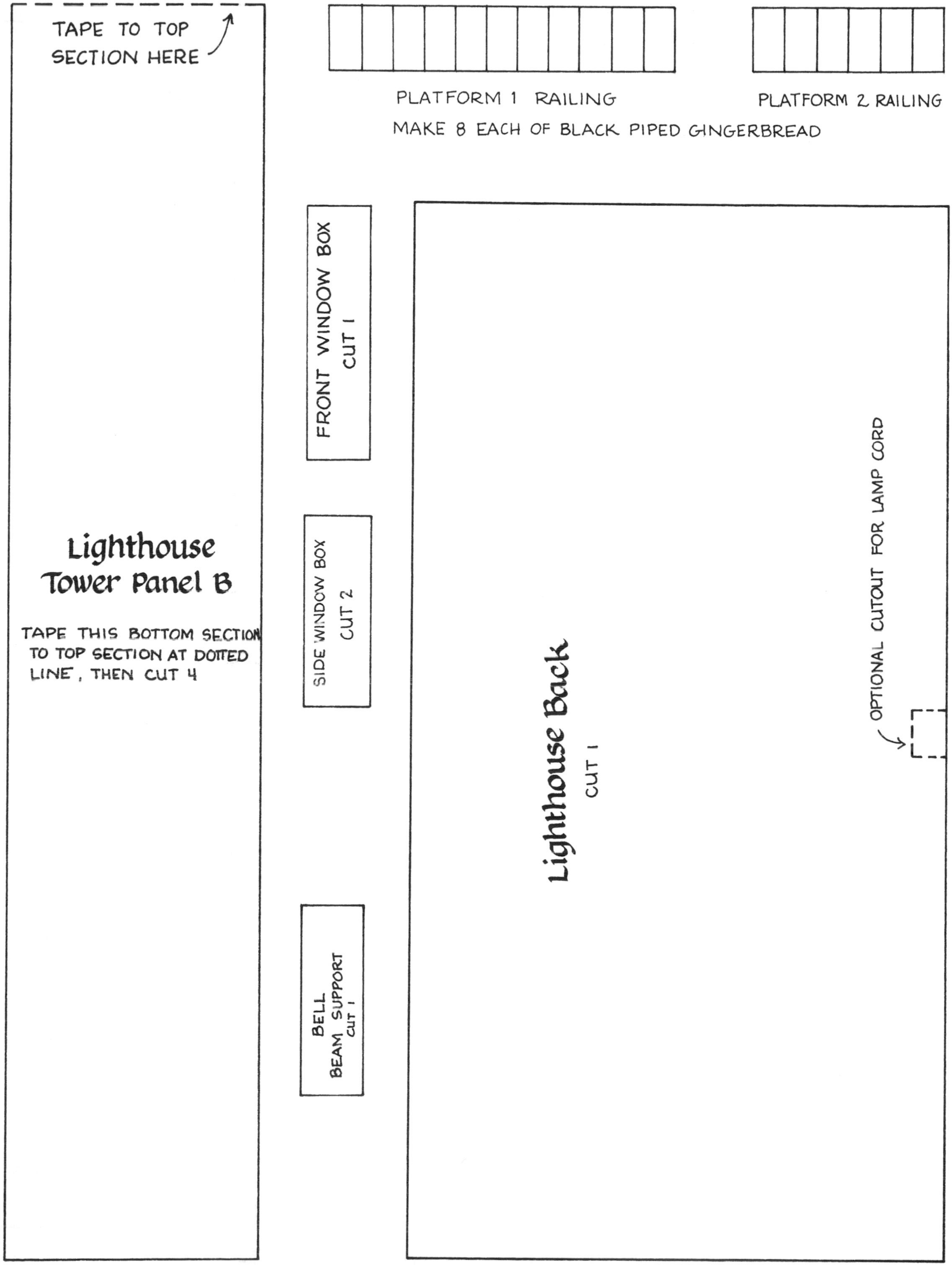

TAPE TO TOP
SECTION HERE

PLATFORM 1 RAILING

PLATFORM 2 RAILING

MAKE 8 EACH OF BLACK PIPED GINGERBREAD

FRONT WINDOW BOX
CUT 1

Lighthouse
Tower Panel B

TAPE THIS BOTTOM SECTION
TO TOP SECTION AT DOTTED
LINE, THEN CUT 4

SIDE WINDOW BOX
CUT 2

OPTIONAL CUTOUT FOR LAMP CORD

Lighthouse Back
CUT 1

BELL
BEAM SUPPORT
CUT 1

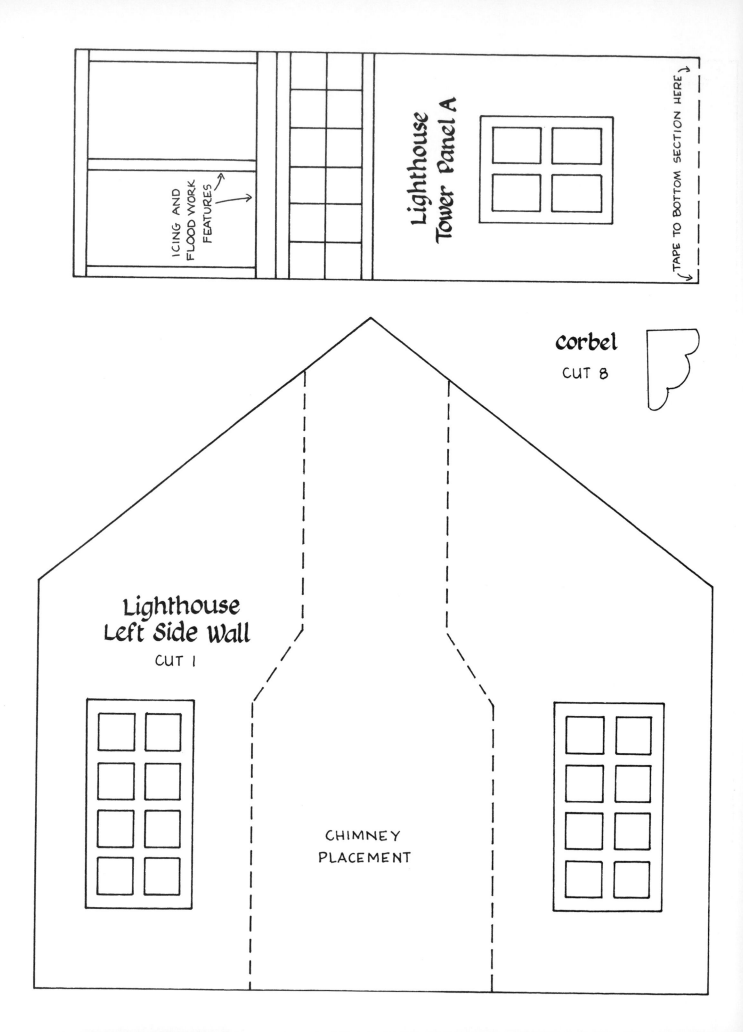

Lighthouse
Tower Panel A

ICING AND FLOOD WORK FEATURES

TAPE TO BOTTOM SECTION HERE

corbel

CUT 8

Lighthouse
Left Side Wall

CUT 1

CHIMNEY
PLACEMENT

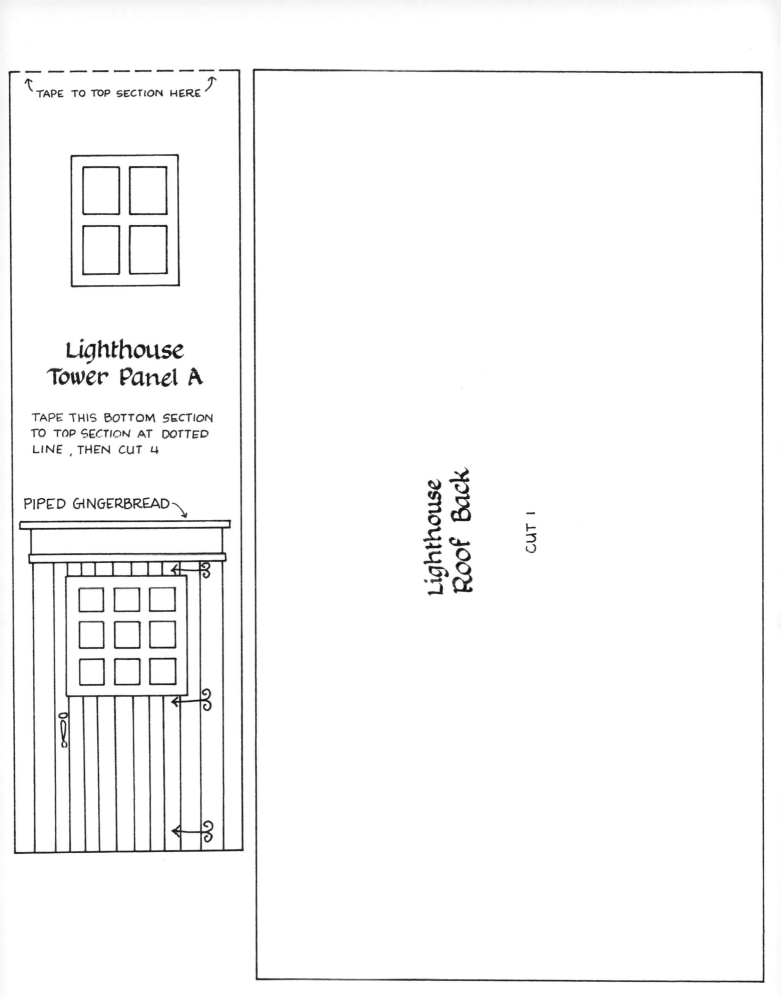

TAPE TO TOP SECTION HERE

Lighthouse
Tower Panel A

TAPE THIS BOTTOM SECTION
TO TOP SECTION AT DOTTED
LINE , THEN CUT 4

PIPED GINGERBREAD

Lighthouse
Roof Back

CUT 1

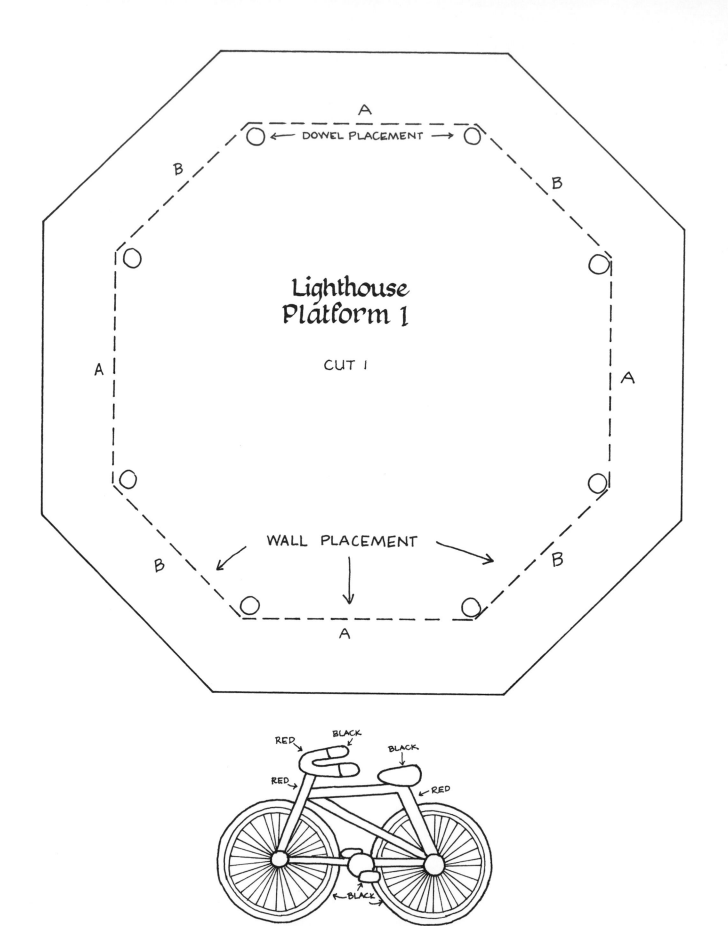

A

← DOWEL PLACEMENT →

B

B

Lighthouse
Platform 1

CUT 1

A

A

B

B

WALL PLACEMENT

A

SUGAR WORK BICYCLE
PIPE SPOKES FIRST USING GRAY ICING

RED

BLACK

BLACK

RED

RED

BLACK

RED SCHOOLHOUSE

1. Lay out and mark board with landscaping features using diagram provided. Drill holes for trees and flag pole using a drill bit to match the diameter of your candy sticks.

2. Cover the board with your choice of paper according to general instructions (page 9) and prepare dough.

3. Make and attach night-light assembly to board (page 13).

4. Make a flag according to general instructions (page 19).

5. Make a bell according to general instructions (page 19).

6. Roll the dough to a ⅛" thickness. Cut and bake the following pieces:

RED SCHOOLHOUSE:

Front - 1 (with windows and door)

Back - 1 (without windows and door)

Sides - 2

Roof - 2

Window trim - 6

Bottom step - 1 (¼" thick)

Top step - 1 (¼" thick)

Porch peak - 1

Porch roof support - 1

Porch roof - 2 (opposites)

Bell tower front and back - 2

Bell tower sides - 2

Bell tower under roof - 1

Bell tower peak - 2

Bell tower roof - 2

Sandbox sides - 4

Sandbox seat - 4

Seesaw - 1

MATERIALS

plywood board 15 x 20 x ½"

paper to cover the board

tape

night-light assembly (see page 13)

1 recipe gingerbread dough

½ recipe green dough

2 recipes royal icing

2 brown candy sticks (porch posts)

4 white candy sticks (bell tower posts)

1 red-and-white candy stick (flag pole)

red powdered food color

paste food colors: red, blue, green

green liquid food color

2 straws

brown sugar

licorice twist

1 pretzel rod

7-ounce package coconut

gum-paste stepping stones

spearmint leaf jelly candies

Wheat Chex® cereal

autumn leaf sugar sequins

Roll green dough ¼" thick. Cut and bake tree pieces using nested 8-point star cutters, six to eight of each size.

7. After baking, rub dry powdered red food coloring into walls, porch peak, and bell tower sections. Brush over it with a dry toothbrush to even out the surface.

8. Decorate window trims with heart and dot design using white icing and a #2 tip. Attach trims to windows with icing and pipe #2 tip icing beads over arches and under sills. Pipe door casing using a #47 tip. Use the notched side to pipe sides and use the flat side to pipe the top. Add a #2 tip line to top of door trim. Pipe door handle and hinges with black icing and a #1 tip. Let dry.

9. Assemble the schoolhouse on the board around the night-light, according to general instructions (page 9). Place front steps with icing.

10. Cut two brown candy sticks to 4⅝" length and glue into holes of top step with icing. See tips for cutting candy sticks (page 19).

11. Assemble the porch roof section separately and let dry.

12. Set bell tower walls in place with icing and shingle the roof with

Schoolhouse Layout Diagram

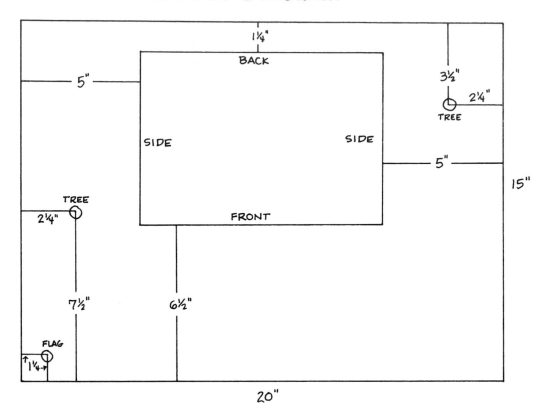

Wheat Chex cereal.

13. Pipe decorative beading on wall seams and under eaves of roof.

14. Cut four white candy sticks to 3" length. Attach one to each corner of bell tower walls with icing, making sure that the tops are level. Let set.

15. Place bell tower under roof on tops of the white candy sticks with icing. Let dry.

16. Insert wire loop from bell up through hole in under roof. Slide a 1" piece of toothpick or skewer through loop to hold bell in place. Pipe icing over toothpick to hold it in place.

17. Assemble bell tower peak on the under roof with icing. Shingle if desired

and pipe decorative icing beads.

18. Make coconut grass by shaking 7 ounces of coconut in a plastic bag with 10 to 20 drops of liquid green food coloring.

19. Ice walkway section of board lightly with white icing. Set gumpaste stepping stones in place. You can cut the gum-paste to fit very easily with scissors.

20. Ice the right side of the board with green icing. Place the first cookie for the tree on that side. Build the sandbox by standing the sides on edge to make a square. Pipe icing on the top edges all the way around; place seat pieces. Fill sand box with brown sugar sand. Sprinkle

coconut grass over the green icing.

21. Ice the left side of the board. Place the first cookie for the tree on the left side. Cover icing with coconut grass. Build seesaw by cutting a 1" piece of pretzel rod. Set in place with icing. Cut two very thin strips of licorice (about $\frac{1}{16}$ x 1"). Stick the ends of the tiny licorice into the holes with icing for seesaw handles. Place seesaw board on pretzel rod base with icing.

22. Build cookie trees as per general instructions (page 14) and place spearmint leaf shrubs with icing.

23. Place flagpole with icing and sprinkle autumn leaf sugar sequins over board.

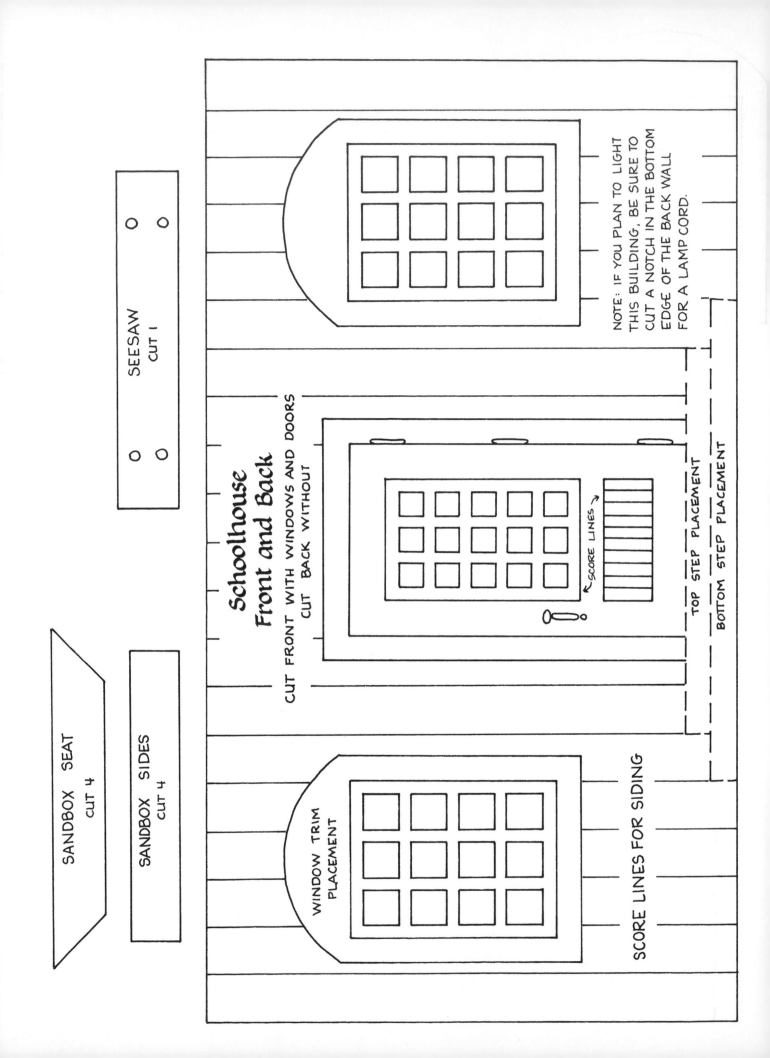

SEESAW
CUT 1

SANDBOX SEAT
CUT 4

SANDBOX SIDES
CUT 4

Schoolhouse
Front and Back
CUT FRONT WITH WINDOWS AND DOORS
CUT BACK WITHOUT

NOTE: IF YOU PLAN TO LIGHT THIS BUILDING, BE SURE TO CUT A NOTCH IN THE BOTTOM EDGE OF THE BACK WALL FOR A LAMP CORD.

WINDOW TRIM PLACEMENT

SCORE LINES →

TOP STEP PLACEMENT

BOTTOM STEP PLACEMENT

SCORE LINES FOR SIDING

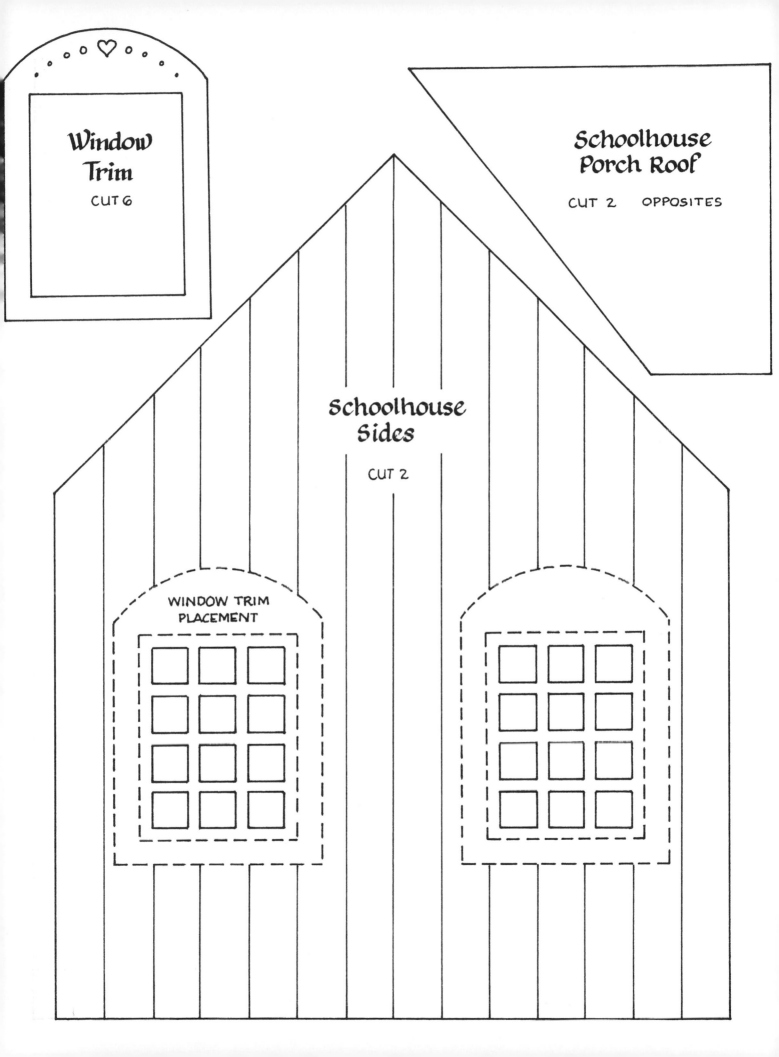

Window Trim

CUT 6

Schoolhouse Porch Roof

CUT 2   OPPOSITES

Schoolhouse Sides

CUT 2

WINDOW TRIM PLACEMENT

Schoolhouse Roof

TAPE PATTERN PIECES TOGETHER AT DOTTED LINE, THEN CUT 2

TAPE TO RIGHT SIDE OF ROOF SECTION HERE

Schoolhouse Bottom Step

POST HOLE

CUT 1
¼" THICK

POST HOLE

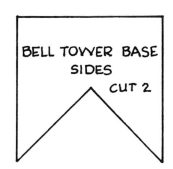

BELL TOWER BASE SIDES

CUT 2

BELL TOWER BASE FRONT & BACK
CUT 2

SCORE LINE ↓

Schoolhouse Roof

TAPE PATTERN PIECES TOGETHER
AT DOTTED LINE, THEN CUT 2

Schoolhouse Bell Tower Under Roof

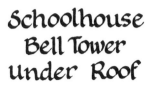

HOLE FOR BELL WIRE

CUT 1

Schoolhouse Bell Tower Roof

CUT 2

BELL TOWER
PEAK
CUT 2

Schoolhouse Top Step

CUT 1
¼" THICK

POST HOLE

POST HOLE

Porch Roof Support
CUT 1

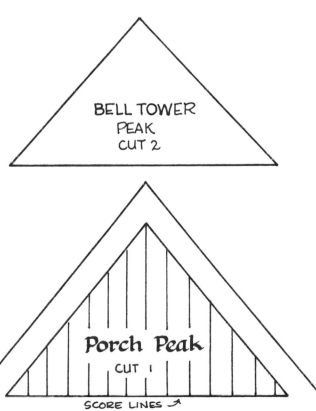

Porch Peak

CUT 1

SCORE LINES ↗

FOUR WINDS FARM

1. Lay out and mark landscaping features on the plywood board using diagram given. Drill ½" holes for apple tree and flagpole placement and ⅜" holes for sign placement.

2. Cover the board with your choice of paper according to general instructions (page 9). Attach night-light assembly to board if desired (page 13) and prepare dough.

3. Roll dough to a ⅛" thickness on nonstick baking parchment. Cut and bake the following pieces:

FOUR WINDS FARM

Front and back - 2 (front with windows and door, back plain with a notch for night-light cord)

Right side wall - 1

Left side wall - 1

Shed addition front and back - 2 (front with door, back without)

Shed addition left side wall - 1

Main roof - 2 (1 with chimney notch, 1 without)

Shed addition roof - 1

Porch roof - 1

Upper Dutch door - 1

Lawn sign - 1

Basket pickets - about 16 per basket

Porch sign - 1

Cider sign - 1

Pie top - 1

Pie bottom - 1

4. Color about 1 cup dough gray. Roll ¼" thick and cut the following pieces:

Chimney - 1

Chimney sides - 2 (opposites)

Chimney back - 1

Chimney top - 1

Score random stone shapes into dough before baking. When cool, mortar the stone chimney sections according to general instructions (page 14). Let dry.

5. Using the flat side of a #47 tip, pipe clapboard siding onto the wall sections, beginning at the bottom edge of each wall and overlapping each row slightly as you work upward. Even out the edges around the windows and doors with a knife after the icing has set about 15 minutes. Let dry.

6. Pipe window trim using green icing and a #6 tip. Let dry.

7. Pipe door handles and hinges using a #1 or #1s tip and black icing.

8. Pipe signs using a #1 or #1s tip. For the "Fresh Apple Cider" sign, write directly on the gingerbread with a green food color pen. Let dry.

9. Make a sugar work flag and brown pumpkin stems according to general instructions (pages 17 and 19). Let dry.

10. To make mason jars, cut a red or purple candy stick into ½" lengths. Pipe a gray lid on each and a white label. Let dry.

11. Make marzipan clay pumpkins (about 12) of varying sizes according to general instructions (page 17).

12. To make apple baskets, pipe icing onto the sides of a jumbo jelly candy. Place the basket pickets all around the jelly candy. Let dry. Pipe brown icing into the top of the basket and fill the basket with miniature red jawbreaker "apples." Add a few green icing leaves. Pipe small bands of icing around the basket as stays. Let dry. Make as many baskets as desired.

13. Outside lantern—use a lemon drop candy as a base. With black icing and a #1 or #1s tip, pipe one line down each side of the lemon drop and two lines equally spaced between them. Pipe a roundish base and top. Let dry. Use black icing to pipe a lantern bracket. Let dry.

14. To make the pumpkin wagon, use brown icing to glue five pretzel sticks together side by side (like a raft), keeping ends even. Make three sections like this (two sides and one bottom). Cut eight pretzel sticks down to 1½" long. Glue four together with brown icing, side by side, for the wagon front and repeat for the wagon back. When all the "rafts" are

dry, attach the sides to the bottom with brown icing, then attach the front and back. Make a handle by making a "T" shape of pretzel sticks and gluing it to the front of the wagon with brown icing. When the wagon has dried, glue in several marzipan pumpkins and strands of Shredded Wheat biscuit for hay with brown icing. Set aside to dry.

15. Make a ladder of pretzel sticks. Cut five 1" pieces of pretzel stick for rungs. Make sure they are even. Use two long (3") pretzel sticks for the sides. Lay one side piece on nonstick parchment, then glue the rungs to the side piece, evenly spaced, with

brown icing. Add a dab of brown icing to the opposite end of each rung and slide the second side into place. Let dry.

16. Make green popcorn balls for trees according to the recipe (page 8). Make a hole in each ball with the handle of a wooden spoon as you make them. This will be where they are attached to the trunk. Using green icing, attach miniature red jawbreakers to the balls as apples. Let dry.

17. Assemble the house around the night-light according to general instructions (page 13). The pieces that are covered with icing will be

FOUR WINDS FARM
LAYOUT DIAGRAM

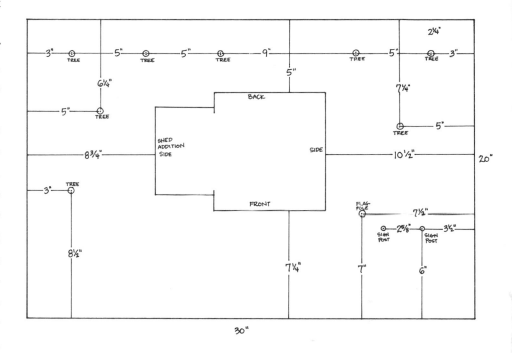

quite heavy, so handle with care. Leave the porch roof off for now. Attach the chimney pieces with icing. Stack a few caramels inside the Dutch door to set the pie on. Glue pie in place with icing.

18. Pave the area in front of the house with gum-paste stepping stones or broken Necco wafers according to general instructions (page 18).

19. Attach the "Fresh Apple Cider" sign to the front window with icing.

20. Using a #18 star tip, pipe a line of icing about ½" under the upper windows, from side to side, on the front of the house. When dry, this will support the porch roof.

21. Pipe #18 star beads along all seams.

22. Build a bench of pretzel sticks under the front window. Stack two short pretzel sticks (about 1" long) perpendicular to the wall at each end of the bench. These will serve as legs. Glue four pretzel sticks across the "legs" as a table top. Place mason jars and an apple basket on the bench with icing.

23. Attach the porch roof to the icing support on the house front with icing. Place the candy stick posts at the same time (an extra pair of hands is very helpful). Let dry.

24. Shingle the roof with Golden Grahams cereal according to general instructions (page 12).

25. Attach the upper part of the Dutch door with icing in an open position.

26. Glue the lemon drop lantern to the wall next to the door with icing, and then attach the lantern bracket just above it with black icing.

27. Attach the "Four Winds Farm" sign to the porch roof with brown icing. Use a prop behind it to hold it up if necessary.

28. Cut two candy cane pieces 2½" long for sign posts and sink them into the drilled holes in the board with icing. Attach the lawn sign to the posts with icing. Glue one red Runts candy to the top of each signpost and top those with a green icing leaf.

29. Cut eight candy sticks to a 5" length for tree trunks. With icing, sink them into the holes drilled in the board.

30. Make coconut grass according to general instructions (page 18). Use two packages of coconut.

31. Cover the grass areas with green icing and coconut grass (do a quarter of the area at a time).

32. With dark brown icing and a #6 tip, pipe bark on the candy sticks to make tree trunks. Run the icing up and down the candy sticks; end some on the ground as roots. Pipe a bit of icing into the hole in each green popcorn ball and set one on each tree trunk. Sprinkle the ground around each tree with a few miniature red jawbreaker apples.

33. Sink the flagpole into its drilled hole with icing.

34. Set the wagon in place, but elevate it on two pretzel sticks. Attach four wagon wheel pasta pieces as wheels.

35. Set the ladder up against an apple tree and set your apple baskets as desired.

Four Winds Farm
Roof

CUT 2 (ONE WITH CHIMNEY NOTCH)

CUT THIS CHIMNEY NOTCH ON RIGHT ROOF ONLY

Four Winds Farm
Shed Addition Roof

CUT 1

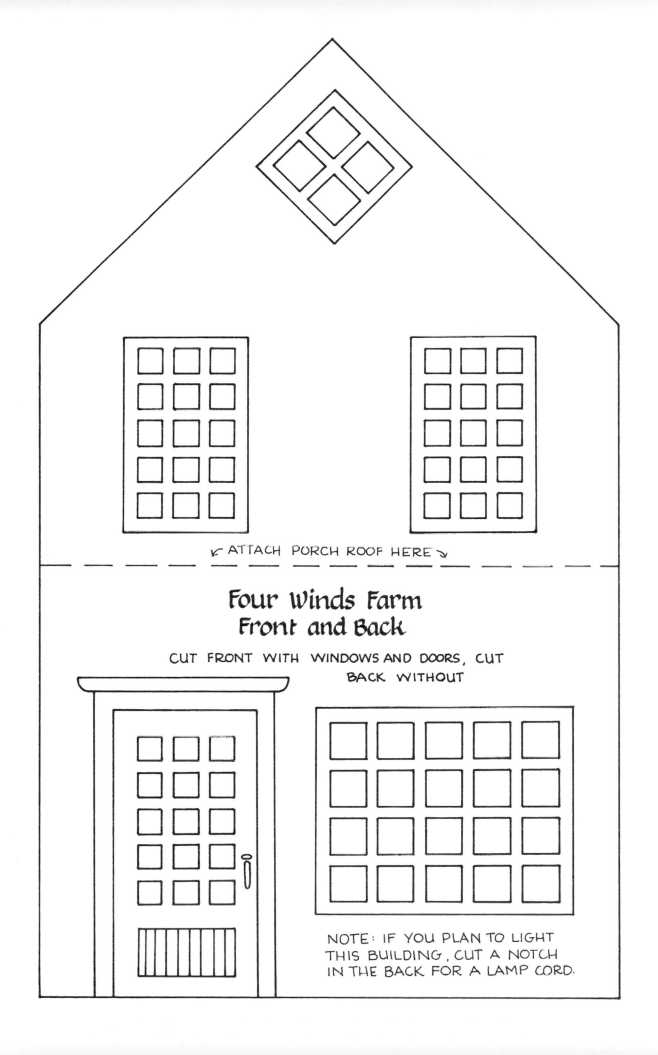

ATTACH PORCH ROOF HERE

Four Winds Farm
Front and Back

CUT FRONT WITH WINDOWS AND DOORS, CUT
BACK WITHOUT

NOTE: IF YOU PLAN TO LIGHT
THIS BUILDING, CUT A NOTCH
IN THE BACK FOR A LAMP CORD.

Four Winds Farm
Left Side Wall

CUT 1

signs

CUT 1 OF EACH

Fresh
APPLE
CIDER

APPLE PIES
APPLE TARTS
APPLE STRUDEL
APPLE BUTTER
APPLE SAUCE
· · · ♡ · · ·

FOUR WINDS FARM

Dutch Door Top

CUT 1
SCORE BOARD LINES

Four winds Farm
Shed Addition
Left Side wall

CUT 1

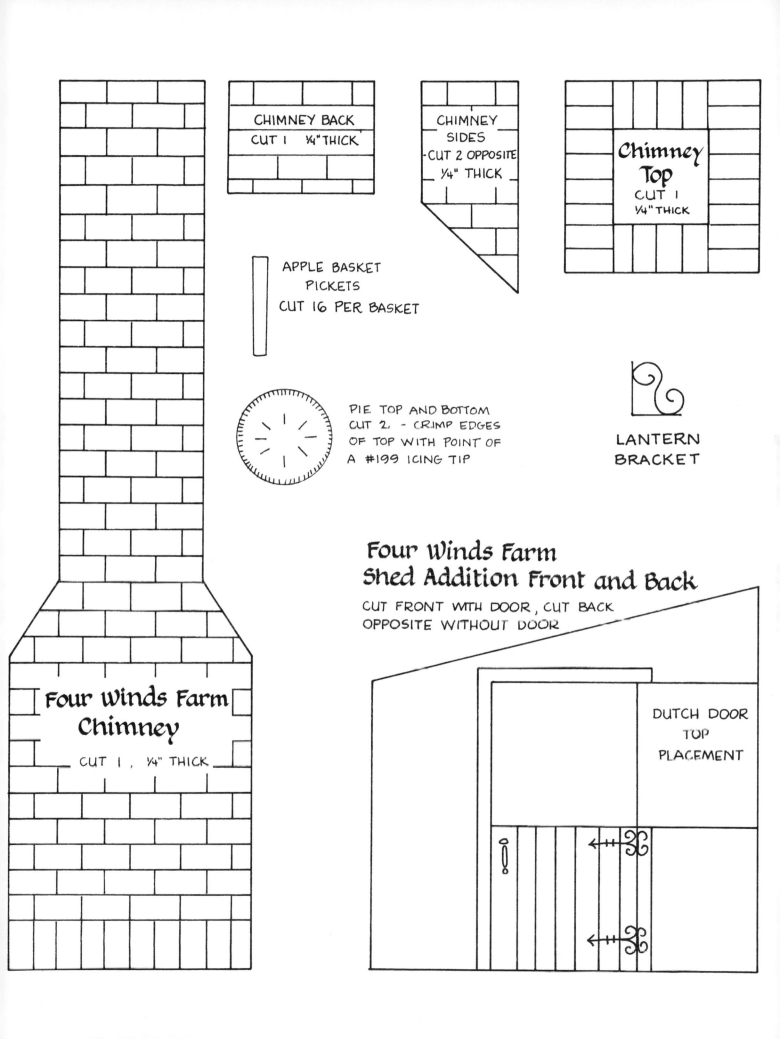

CHIMNEY BACK
CUT 1   ¼" THICK

CHIMNEY
SIDES
CUT 2 OPPOSITE
¼" THICK

Chimney
Top
CUT 1
¼" THICK

APPLE BASKET
PICKETS
CUT 16 PER BASKET

PIE TOP AND BOTTOM
CUT 2 - CRIMP EDGES
OF TOP WITH POINT OF
A #199 ICING TIP

LANTERN
BRACKET

Four Winds Farm
Chimney

CUT 1 , ¼" THICK

Four Winds Farm
Shed Addition Front and Back
CUT FRONT WITH DOOR, CUT BACK
OPPOSITE WITHOUT DOOR

DUTCH DOOR
TOP
PLACEMENT

Four Winds Farm
Porch Roof

CUT 1

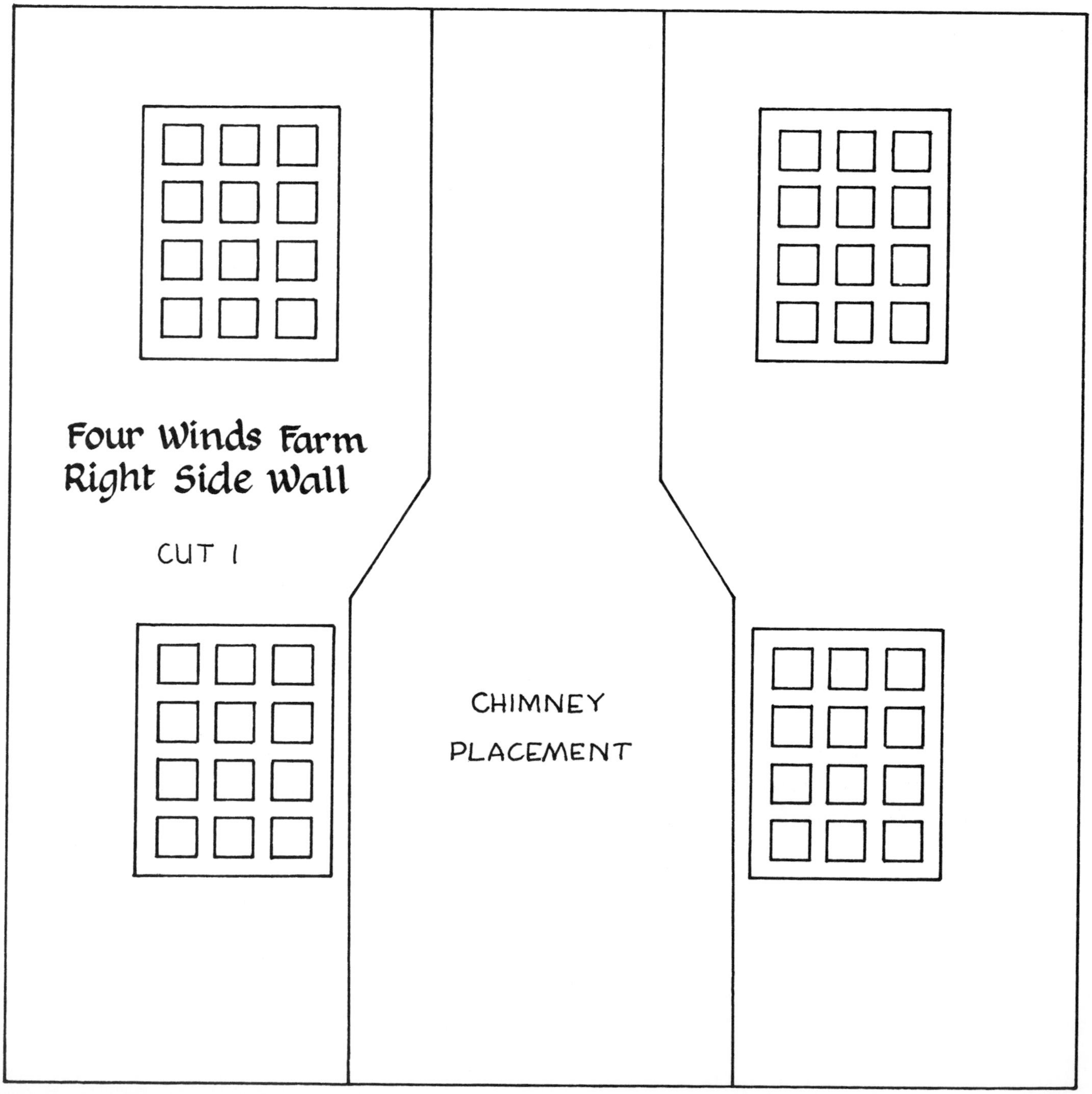

Four Winds Farm
Right Side Wall

CUT 1

CHIMNEY
PLACEMENT

HAUNTED HOUSE

1. Lay out and mark board with landscaping features using diagram provided. Drill holes for wooden dowels using a drill bit to match the diameter of the dowels (¼").

2. Cover the board with your choice of paper according to the general instructions (page 9) and prepare dough and icing (page 8).

3. Make sugar work using patterns given for spiderwebs (using a #1 tip) and porch railing (using a #2 tip). With black icing and a #1 tip, pipe three bats—one each on 3" lengths of fine wire. Pipe a cat using a #2 tip and black icing. Pipe pumpkin stems using a #1 tip and brown icing. See general instructions (page 17). Let dry.

4. Make flood work ghosts using patterns given. See general instructions (page 16). Let dry. Ghost faces can be piped on with black icing and a #1s tip or drawn on using food coloring markers (see source list).

5. Roll the dough to a ⅛" thickness. Cut and bake the following pieces:

HAUNTED HOUSE

Front - 1

Side brackets - 2 (opposites)

Bay window front - 1

Bay window side wall - 2 (opposites)

Porch roof bracket - 1

Porch roof - 1

Porch floor support - 1

Porch floor - 1

Bottom step - 1 (¼" thick)

Second step - 1 (¼" thick)

Upper shutters - 2

Lower shutters - 2

6. Prepare ½ cup gingerbread dough for piping (page 14). Fill a pastry bag with a #6 tip attached. Pipe random tree branches—about 8 to 10" each including the trunk. The trunk portion should be four to six lines of piped dough spreading out to branches. Make four to six pieces like this. Bake until branches are deep brown. Pipe "iron" fences using a #4 tip and black piping dough, and bake 10 minutes.

7. Using royal blue and violet powdered food colors, lightly rub color into baked wall and bracket pieces with your fingers. Some pieces will have darker smudges than others. This adds to the character of the house.

8. Rub black powdered food color into the shutters and brown and purple powdered food color into steps.

9. Tint about 2 cups of royal icing tan using brown paste food color. With a #2 tip, pipe the tan icing on all window mullions and casings. Using a #4 tip, pipe around the door casing and pipe a trim line across the tops of all the window casings.

10. With a small icing spatula or butter knife, spread black icing on all roof sections so it has a rough sur-

face. Then pipe around the edges with black icing using a #2 tip. Let dry.

11. Using white icing and a #1 tip, pipe a spiderweb on the top right window section of the bay window front piece. Pipe the spider with black icing. Let dry.

12. Glue the upper shutters in place on the center window with tan icing.

13. Use a #1 tip and black icing to pipe the "ironwork" under the attic window on the right side of the house. Let dry.

14. Run your fingers over the paper on the baseboard to find the drilled holes. Use a knife or scissor points to break the paper into the holes.

15. Sink the dowels into the drilled holes with the two tallest ones in the two center holes, and the shorter ones in the end holes. They will be used to stabilize the house facade.

16. Using tan icing and a #4 tip, pipe beads on the fronts of the dowels and a line of icing on the board just in front of the dowels. Stand the house front in the line of icing on the board and attach it to the dowels.

17. Attach the side brackets to the board and back side edges of the house front with tan icing.

18. Attach the bay window side walls to the front wall with tan icing. Attach the porch roof bracket at the far left edge of the house front, keeping it at the same level as the top angle of the bay window side walls.

19. Attach bay window front with tan icing.

20. Glue porch support to baseboard

HAUNTED HOUSE LAYOUT DIAGRAM

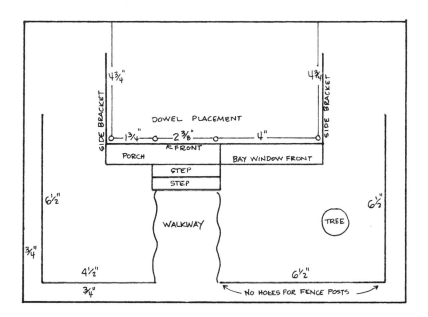

and bay window side wall with tan icing. Attach porch floor.

21. Glue bottom step in place, then second step, with tan icing.

22. Attach porch roof to front wall, porch roof brackets and bay window with tan icing.

23. Glue on the bay window shutters with icing.

24. Measure and cut two lengths of brown candy stick for porch posts. Set them in place with tan icing. Rub brown powdered color on the porch railing sugar work and set it between the porch posts with tan icing.

25. Pipe a thin line of white icing on the straight edges of the sugarwork spiderwebs and set them in place— one on the roof and one in the corner of the porch. Set ghosts in place with

white icing. Set bat wires in place.

26. Handle your tree pieces carefully and stack the trunk sections so the branches spread nicely to each side. Wrap the lower part of the trunk with a piece of masking tape, then slip the trunk into a 1¼" diameter cardboard tube. Being careful of the branches, fill the tube with tan icing. Prop up on a cookie sheet with cans to dry. The tree is top-heavy, so be sure to support it very well.

27. Prepare an icing bag with dark brown icing and a #6 tip. Ice the board with tan icing, placing a large dollop where the tree will be. Set the tree in place. Use a small icing spatula to pull the icing from the dollop up the sides of the tree. Use the dark brown icing bag to pipe lines up and down the tree trunk, with some end-

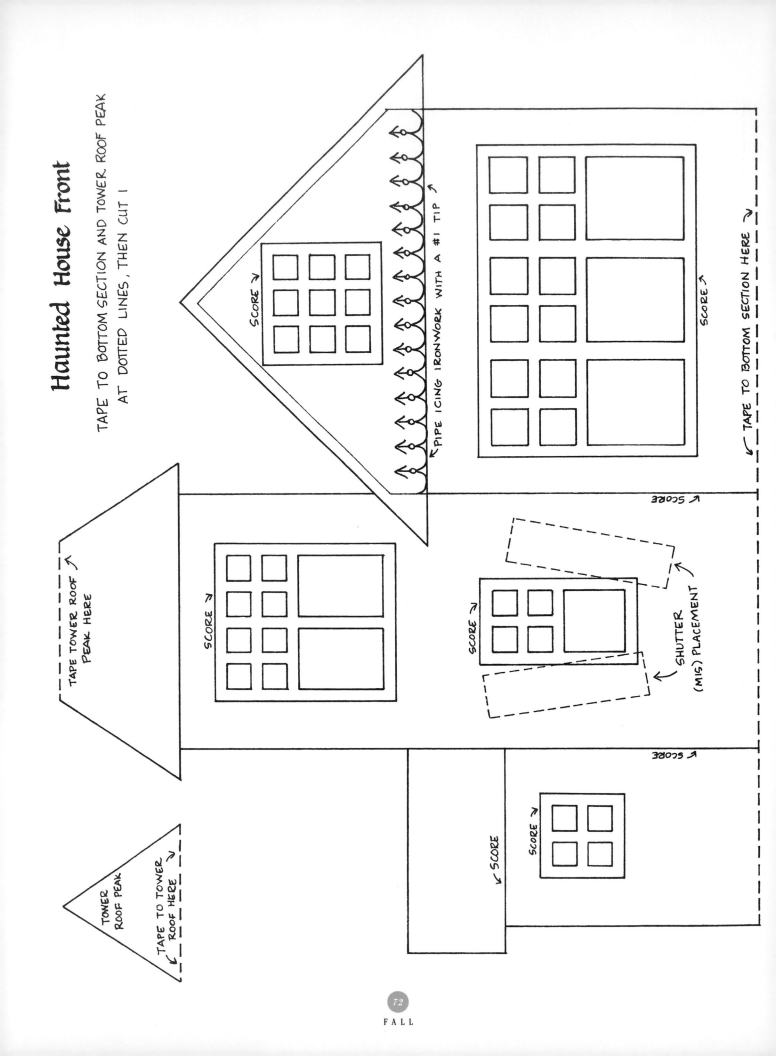

Haunted House Front

TAPE TO BOTTOM SECTION AND TOWER ROOF PEAK
AT DOTTED LINES, THEN CUT 1

PIPE ICING IRONWORK WITH A #1 TIP

SCORE

SCORE

SCORE

SCORE

SCORE

SCORE

SCORE

TAPE TO BOTTOM SECTION HERE

TAPE TO BOTTOM SECTION HERE

TAPE TOWER ROOF PEAK HERE

SHUTTER (MIS) PLACEMENT

TOWER ROOF PEAK

TAPE TO TOWER ROOF HERE

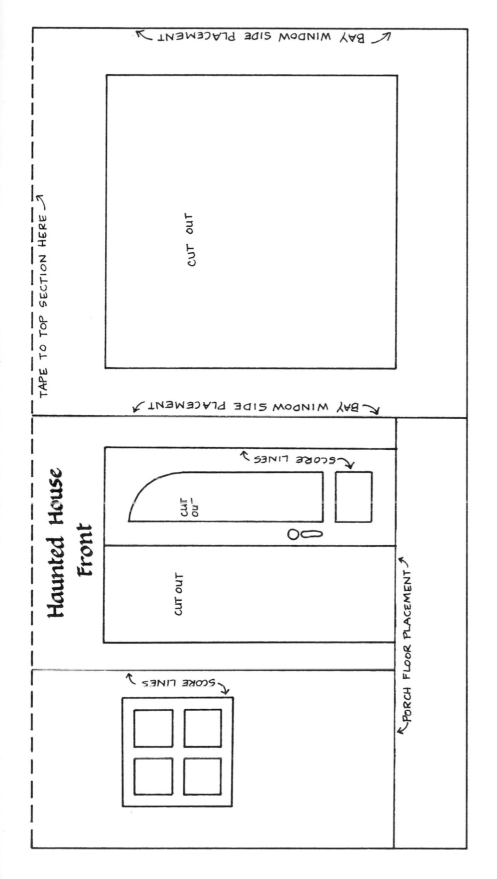

ing on the ground as roots.

NOTE: Your tree is very fragile at this point, so try not to bump the board in any way.

28. Set the walkway in place using broken crackers.

29. Set the fence sections into the tan icing on the board and also attach them to each other at the corners with black icing.

30. Make pumpkins by rolling three different size balls of orange marzipan or candy clay and scoring lines in each from top to bottom around the balls. Poke a toothpick in the top of each to make a hole for the stem. Attach a stem on each with a tiny dab of brown icing. Set pumpkins in place.

31. Set the cat in place.

32. Pull apart the large Shredded Wheat biscuits to get some clusters of long strands to use for dried grass and set them around your house with tan icing. Sprinkle the yard with broken Shredded Wheat and some autumn leaf sugar sequins. Let dry overnight.

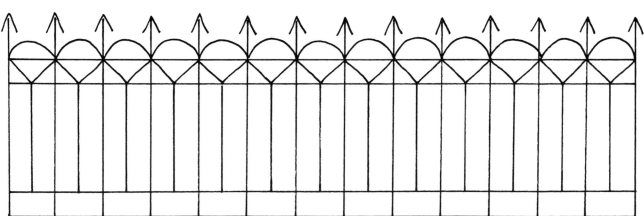

HAUNTED HOUSE FENCE - PIPED GINGERBREAD - #4 TIP
MAKE 3 SECTIONS 6½" LONG AND 1 SECTION 4½" LONG

Sugar Work

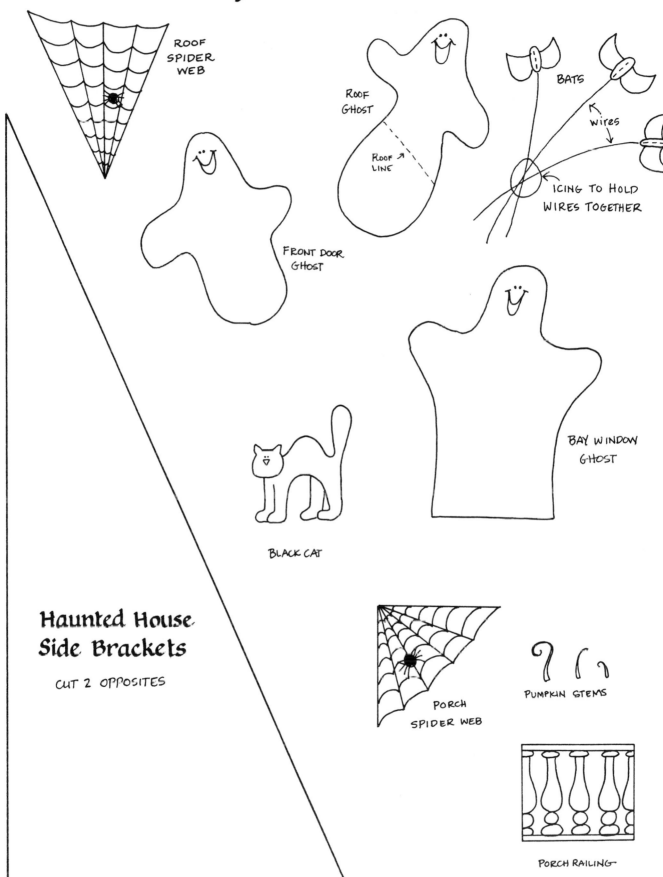

ROOF SPIDER WEB

ROOF GHOST

ROOF LINE

BATS

wires

ICING TO HOLD WIRES TOGETHER

FRONT DOOR GHOST

BAY WINDOW GHOST

BLACK CAT

Haunted House Side Brackets

CUT 2 OPPOSITES

PORCH SPIDER WEB

PUMPKIN STEMS

PORCH RAILING

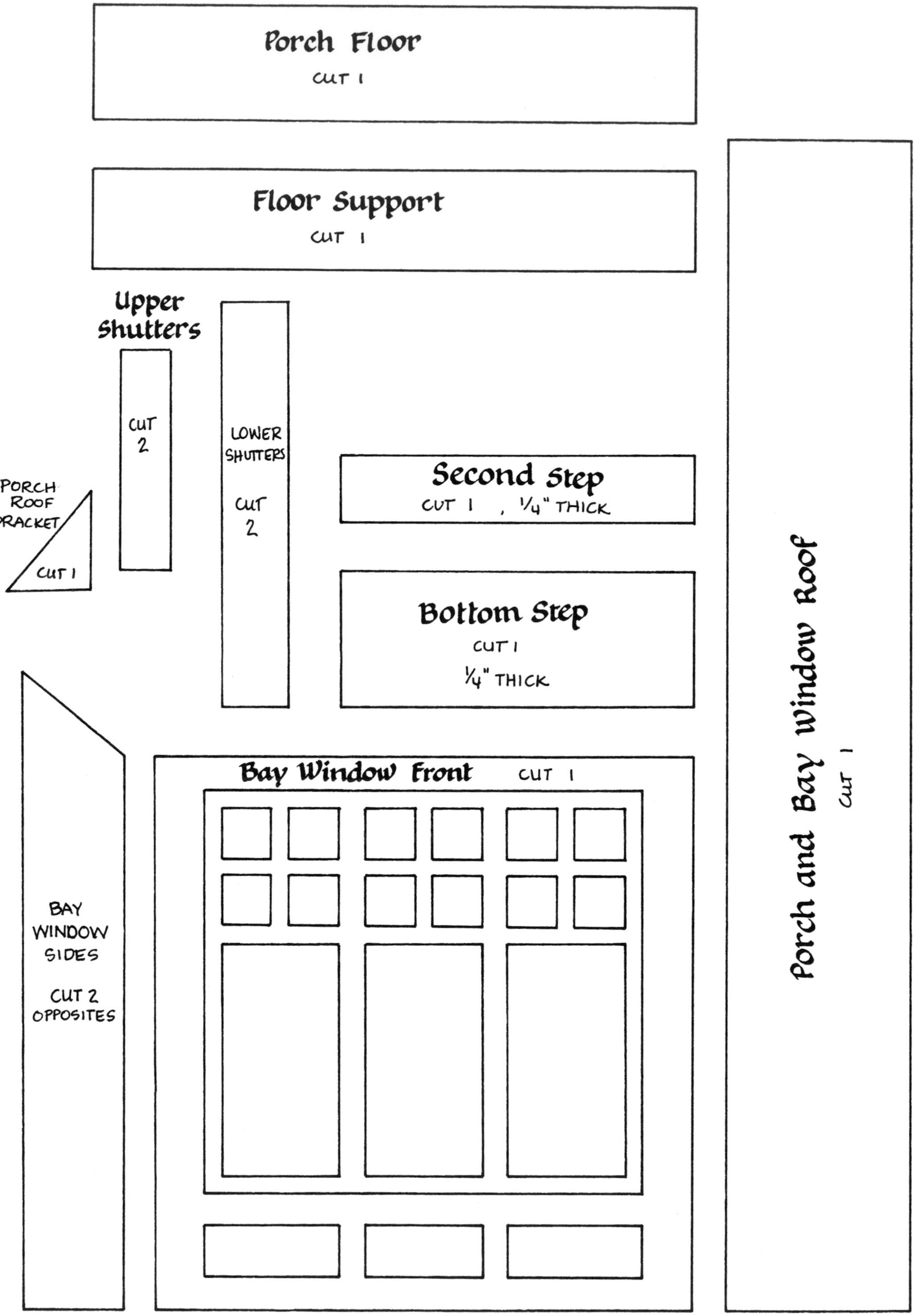

Porch Floor

CUT 1

Floor Support

CUT 1

Upper Shutters

CUT 2

LOWER SHUTTERS

CUT 2

PORCH ROOF BRACKET

CUT 1

Second Step

CUT 1 , 1/4" THICK

Bottom Step

CUT 1

1/4" THICK

BAY WINDOW SIDES

CUT 2 OPPOSITES

Bay Window Front   CUT 1

Porch and Bay Window Roof

CUT 1

VICTORIAN CHRISTMAS COTTAGE

1. Mark and drill (⅜" bit) holes for fence posts (see layout diagram).

2. Using paper and tape, cover the plywood board as if wrapping a present. Attach night-light assembly if desired.

3. Cut and bake the following pieces:

VICTORIAN CHRISTMAS COTTAGE

Front - 1

Back - 1

Side walls - 2

Front roof - 1

Back roof - 1

Gable roof - 2

Fence pickets - 60

Note: The easiest way to cut these is to use a straight edge and cut two long cuts 2" apart, then 60 thin cuts (¼") from the 2" strip of dough. Make sure all are laid out straight before baking. Or use pretzel sticks.

4" fence rails - 8

5" fence rails - 4

Gate - 1

Arbor - 1 (bake on parchment wrapped around a 3" diameter can set in a cradle of aluminum foil)

4. Attach lace over windows with icing if you want curtains.

5. Pipe door handle and hinges with black icing.

MATERIALS

plywood board 15 x 15 x ½"

paper to cover board

tape

night-light assembly (see page 13)

1 recipe gingerbread dough

2 recipes royal icing

1 black gumdrop (Crows®)

sliced almonds for shingles

4 caramels

14 spearmint leaves jelly candies

2 sugar cones

7 8" candy canes

green sugar sequins

red nonpareils

gum-paste stepping stones (page 18) or black, brown, and purple Necco® wafers

1 thin pretzel stick

green sugar crystals

paste food color: orange, black, and green

red gum for shutters

toothpicks

red and white miniature jawbreakers

6. Assemble the cottage on the covered board around the light, leaving about 2" of space between light and wall (as per general instructions).

7. Make the trees of your choice (page 14).

8. Make snowman (page 17).

9. Make shovel (page 17).

10. To make fence sections, lay two 4" fence rails parallel to each other 1¾" apart. Pipe icing on both rails. Lay fence pickets evenly into icing about 1⁄16" apart. Repeat with other fence sections to make four 4" sections and two 5" sections.

11. Shingle roof as per general instructions (page 11) using sliced almonds as shingles.

12. Prepare shutters by cutting 12 sticks of red gum to ½" wide by 2" long. Attach shutters to window sides with icing. Pipe shutter dogs on bottom of shutters with black icing.

13. Make garlands under windows and around door frame as per general instructions (page 17). Pipe a bow of red icing at top of garland over door.

14. Make packages by cutting caramels into different sizes and piping "strings" on them with a #1 tip. Let dry.

15. Pipe beading along roof ridges (main roof and gable). Set red and white miniature jawbreakers alternately—one on each bead.

16. Pipe string work as per general instructions (page 16) around all eaves of roof.

17. Pipe beading around all eaves.

18. Prepare stones for walkway by rolling and cutting dark gray gum paste into various stone shapes, some larger than others. Or use broken Necco wafers (black, brown, and purple) and pave walkway as per general instructions (page 18).

19. Cut candy canes to size for fence posts. (See tips for cutting candy canes, page 19.) You'll need six 3" pieces and four 4¾" pieces.

20. Find the holes drilled in the board by running a finger over the paper on the board, breaking the paper and pushing the paper into the holes.

21. Using an icing spatula, ice the board to a depth of ¼". Place spearmint leaf shrubs, trees, snowman, and packages in front of the door and snow shovel beside the door.

22. Place candy cane fence posts and arbor posts in drilled holes (add extra icing if needed). Attach fence sections to fence posts with icing. Attach gate at walkway. Pipe icing to tops of tall posts. Place arbor top.

23. Pipe tops on fence posts. Add small candy balls if desired.

24. Make garlands on the front fence sections according to the general instructions (page 17).

CHRISTMAS COTTAGE LAYOUT DIAGRAM

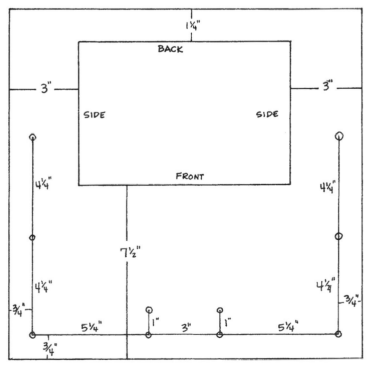

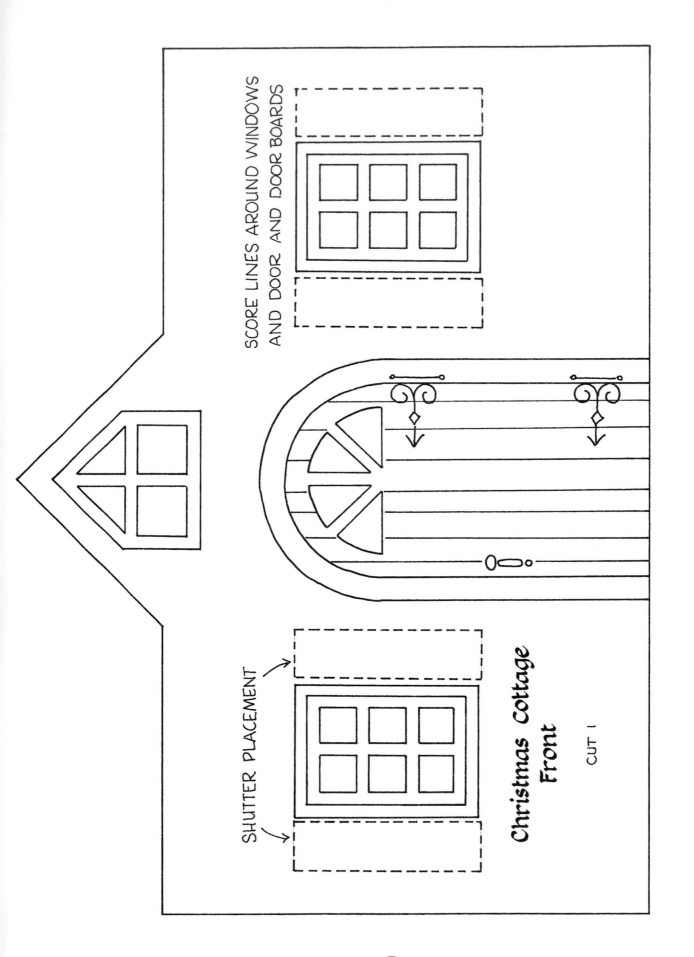

SCORE LINES AROUND WINDOWS
AND DOOR AND DOOR BOARDS

SHUTTER PLACEMENT

Christmas Cottage Front

CUT 1

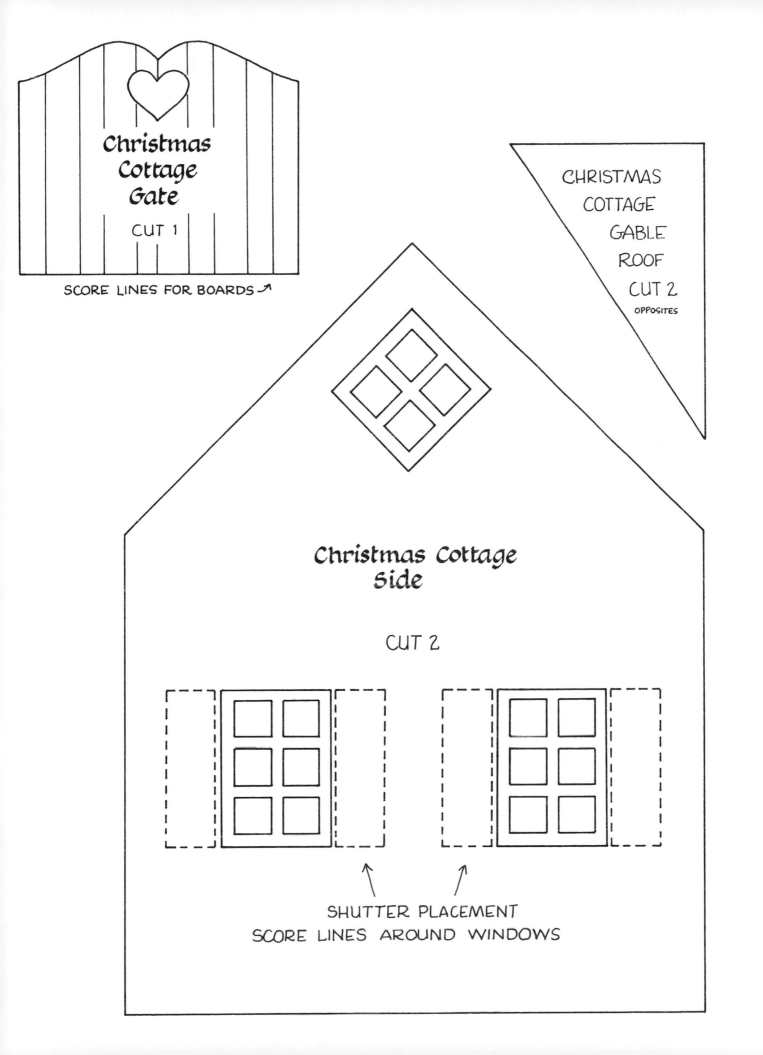

Christmas
Cottage
Gate

CUT 1

SCORE LINES FOR BOARDS ↗

CHRISTMAS
COTTAGE
GABLE
ROOF
CUT 2
OPPOSITES

Christmas Cottage
Side

CUT 2

SHUTTER PLACEMENT
SCORE LINES AROUND WINDOWS

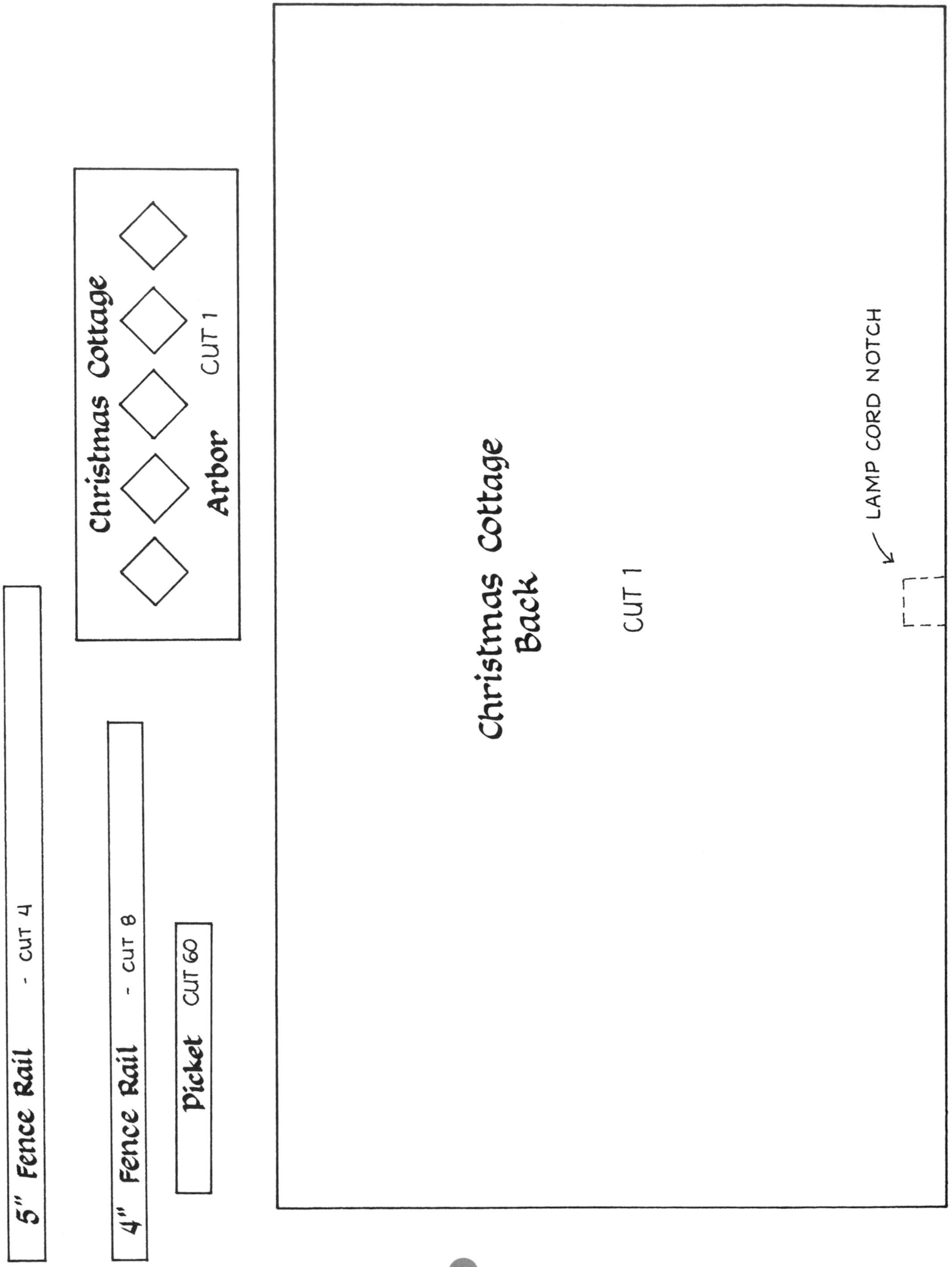

Christmas Cottage

Arbor

CUT 1

5" Fence Rail — CUT 4

4" Fence Rail — CUT 8

Picket CUT 60

Christmas Cottage Back

CUT 1

LAMP CORD NOTCH

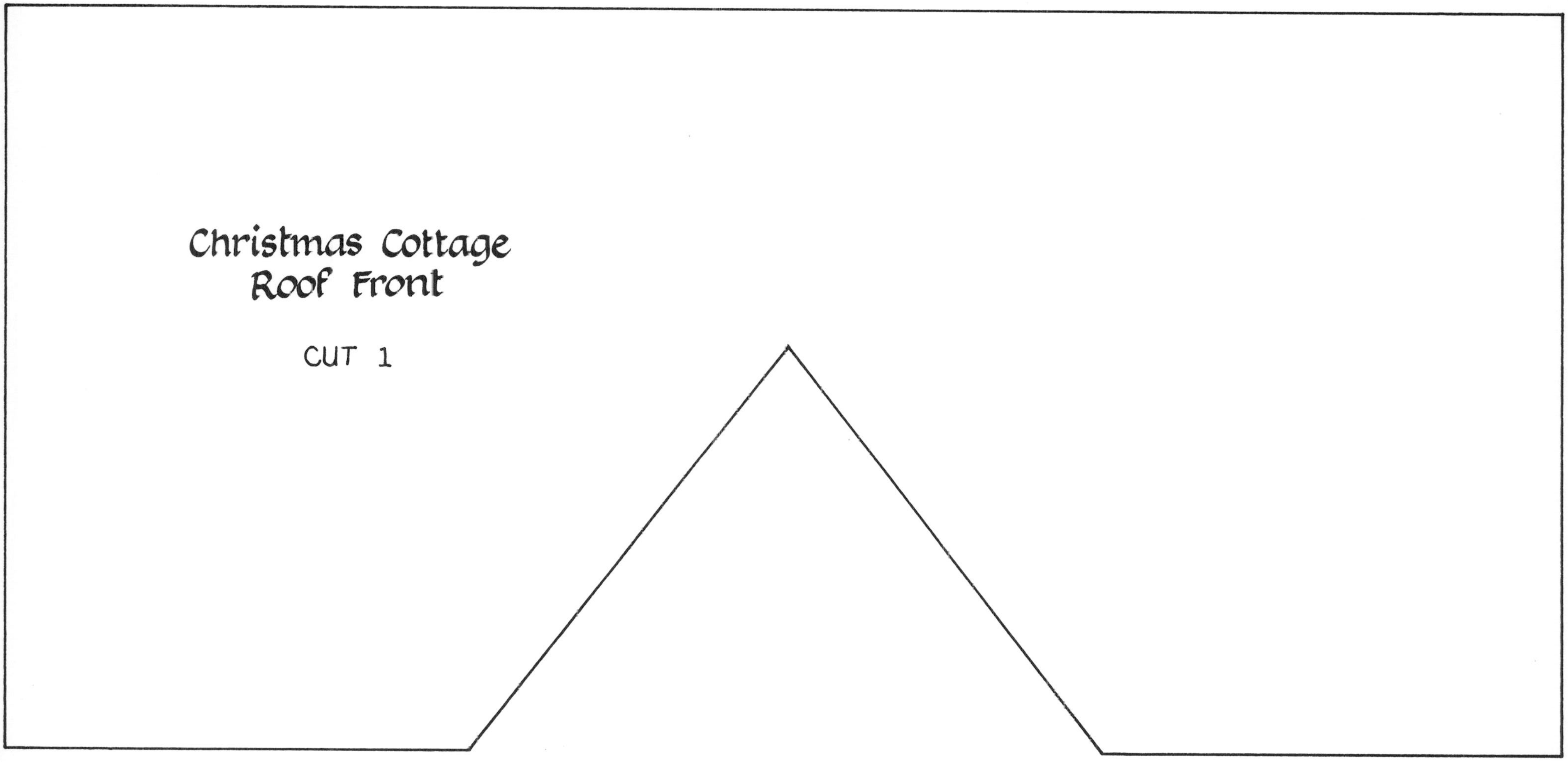

Christmas Cottage
Roof Front

CUT 1

Christmas Cottage
Roof Back

CUT 1

SANTA'S SLEIGH

Note: Please do not try this as a first project.

Success in building this project will come from accurate cutting, careful assembly, and letting each component dry thoroughly before adding the next. It can only be expected to hold its own weight if the icing is allowed to dry between steps. Keep in mind that this project will take two to five days to build because of drying time.

1. Cover the board with your choice of paper according to general instructions (page 9).

2. Make two recipes of gingerbread dough and divide each in half. Color one part red, one black, one green, and leave one brown.

3. Roll the red dough to ⅛" thick on nonstick baking parchment. Cut and bake the following pieces:

SANTA'S SLEIGH

Sides - 2 (opposites)

Bottom - 1

Front - 1

Back - 1

Slats - 12

Toy shelf - 1

Toy shelf brace - 2

Santa's arm - 2 (opposites)—save

MATERIALS

plywood board 9 x 42 x ½"

paper to cover the board

tape

2 recipes gingerbread dough—divide each recipe in half to make four dough colors: red, black, green, plain

4–5 recipes royal icing

1 recipe white chocolate clay

3 Styrofoam eggs 2¼" long

1 Styrofoam ball 3" diameter

paste food colors: black, brown, red, green, blue

toothpicks

bamboo skewer

Starburst® fruit chews

white gum balls

yellow Runts® candies

green jumbo jelly candies

star sugar sequins

silver dragées

holly leaf sugar sequins

red licorice laces

large and small gum balls

tiny red ball candies (Wilton® peanut sprinkles)

the extra dough for Santa's suit.

4. Roll the black dough to ¼" thick. Cut and bake the following:

Sleigh runners - 2 (opposites)—make sure the bottom edge is flat.

Center under-carriage brace - 1

Front and back under-carriage brace - 2

5. Roll the black dough to ⅛" thick. Cut and bake the following pieces:

Under-carriage platform - 1

Sleigh seat - 1

Sleigh seat front - 1

Interior seat brace - 1

6. Roll the plain gingerbread dough ¼" thick on nonstick parchment. Cut and bake the reindeer pieces as follows:

Reindeer #1, #4, #8:

    Front - 3

    Back - 3

Reindeer #2, #5:

    Front - 2

    Back - 2

    Face - 2

Reindeer #3, #6, #7:

    Front - 3

    Back - 3

Note: It is wise to make extra reindeer parts in case of breakage.

7. Roll the green dough to ¼" thick on nonstick parchment. Cut three each of the smallest nested stars for a tree and five tree-top triangles. Bake as directed. (See "Trees" under general instructions, page 14.)

8. Make the toys as follows:

A. Make two or three jack-in-the-boxes according to directions in Geppetto's Toy Shop (page 107).

B. Make three sugar work sailboats, five to six small soldiers, and two to three large soldiers according to sugar work directions (page 16) and using patterns given.

C. Dollhouses: make two dollhouses by cutting pink Starburst candies into a house shape. Add gum for roof pieces and colored nonpareils to the edge of the roof with icing. Stick a tiny square slice of yellow Starburst to the front of the house to make a window. With a #1 tip, pipe on brown icing for shutters and a door. Make a doorknob with one white nonpareil. Let dry.

D. Make a teddy bear out of raw gingerbread dough. You can either bake him or just let him dry. Pipe a face with black icing and a #1 tip.

E. Use large and small gum balls as balls.

F. For wrapped presents, use hard candies in various sizes and shapes and pipe bows of icing in different colors. Add holly leaves and berries (nonpareils) to the bow centers if desired. Let dry.

9. Stack up the green star cookies with the largest on bottom to smallest on top. Use green icing between to stick them together. Set the tree-top triangles in place with green icing, having vertical edges touching and triangles radiating outward. Top with a star cut from a flattened yellow Starburst candy. Let dry.

10. To make lanterns for the front of the sleigh, cut a yellow Starburst candy in half. Use black icing and a #1s tip to pipe a "Y" shape on three sides of the candy rectangle. Pipe a line down each corner and cover the top and bottom with black icing. Let dry.

11. Pipe icing curls and dots on sleigh sides and front. Let dry.

12. Assemble the sleigh. Place bottom facedown. Use a #6 tip and white icing to attach the sides to the bottom (they should sit on top of the bottom piece, not next to it). Use soup cans to help hold it up. Attach the front and back pieces with icing, making sure the edges all match. Let dry thoroughly. (See fig. 1)

13. Carefully turn the sleigh over and rest it upside down on a towel. Ice the edges of the curves and attach the slats to span the width from side to side, and also ice the edges between the slats. Let dry. (See fig. 2)

14. Carefully turn the sleigh right side up and attach the seat supports to the inside with icing. The shorter one goes toward the back and the taller one goes toward the front of the seat area. Place the seat on the supports with icing.

15. Build the toy shelf on top of the seat. Attach one toy shelf support to the inside back of the sleigh and attach the other toward the front edge of the toy shelf. Glue the toy shelf on the supports with icing. Let dry.

16. Roughly mark the placement of the sleigh runners on the covered board. Ice that section of the board about ⅜" deep. With black icing, pipe beads down each side edge of center under-brace. Stand center under brace in the icing snow at the center of where the runners will be. Stand one runner at a 90-degree angle in the snow as if putting up walls of a house. (See fig. 3)

17. Pipe icing on the side edges of front and back under brace sections and stand them 90 degrees to the runner in the icing snow, but tilt the front one toward the back and the back one toward the front. (See fig. 3) Stand the second runner in the icing snow against the under-brace pieces.

18. Use black icing to place the under-carriage platform across the center under brace from runner to runner. Let this assembly dry thoroughly.

19. Ice the top surface of the under-carriage piece and carefully place the sleigh on top. Use black icing to fill the small gaps between the sleigh and the runners.

20. Slightly flatten the sides and bottom of two 2¼" Styrofoam eggs. To make toy bags, roll green dough about ⅛" thick. Cut a 6" circle of dough and wrap it around the Styrofoam egg. Pinch in the top and carefully adjust the folds. If the dough tears a little, just patch it by pushing the edges back together. Make two bags like this and glue

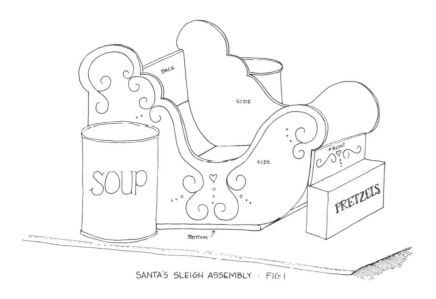

SANTA'S SLEIGH ASSEMBLY - FIG.1

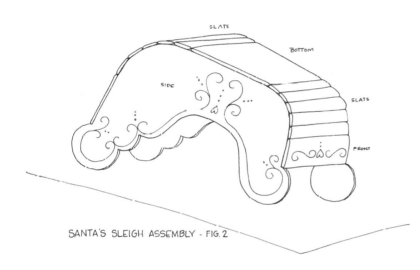

SANTA'S SLEIGH ASSEMBLY - FIG. 2

SANTA'S SLEIGH
RUNNER AND UNDER BRACE ASSEMBLY
FIG. 3

them side by side on the toy shelf of the sleigh with icing.

21. For Santa:

A. Use a 2¼" Styrofoam egg, flattened slightly on the bottom, as a base for a body. Roll red dough ⅛" thick and wrap it around the egg to cover. Trim off excess and smooth seams with your fingers.

B. Cover the hand section of the gingerbread arms with green dough and cover arm section with red dough. Attach arms to body by pushing a piece of bamboo skewer through body section at shoulder, then attaching an arm to each side with icing. Have the skewer go through the hole in each arm. Cover the hole with a plug of red gingerbread dough.

C. Make Santa's head out of marzipan clay or white chocolate clay. Color a bit of clay to the skin tone of your choice and roll a ball the size of a walnut. Make a nose and round rosy cheeks and press in place. Pipe black eye dots. Make a hat of red dough and attach with icing. Attach head to body with icing and a toothpick for support.

D. Use a #14 star tip to pipe white icing around sleeve edges, down body front, hair, beard, hat trim, and pompom. Pipe his mustache with a #6 tip. Put a small red ball candy in under the mustache for a mouth. Set silver dragée buttons down his front. Place two green leaf sequins and three red nonpareil berries on his hat with icing. Let dry. Then set Santa on the seat with icing.

22. Make the lap quilt by rolling a piece of white chocolate clay to less than ⅛" thick. Cut a rectangle about 4 x 5". Tint a piece of white chocolate clay red. It will become quite soft as you work the color into it, so let it rest in the refrigerator for a few minutes as needed. Roll the tinted clay very thin on wax paper or non-stick parchment. Cut small squares (¼") and stick them to the 4 x 5" rectangle of white clay in a simple pattern. When the pattern is done, place a piece of wax paper over the quilt and roll it lightly with a rolling pin to stick the two colors together.

23. Place a 3" Styrofoam ball into the bottom of the sleigh in front of Santa. Carefully drape the quilt over the ball, having a corner hang nicely over the side of the sleigh. It should look like it covers Santa's lap.

24. Fill the sleigh and toy bags with the toys made earlier and glue them in place with icing. Attach the small tree into the front part of the sleigh as well. Attach lanterns to

sleigh front with icing and top with a star sugar sequin on each lantern. Let dry.

25. Glue reindeer fronts and backs together with brown icing, being very careful of their antlers, as they are fragile. Make sure the hole through their centers is free of icing remnants. Let dry.

26. Pipe reindeer faces with black icing and a #1 tip. Let dry.

27. Carefully lay out the back row of reindeer (#2, #4, #6, #8) on nonstick parchment. Cut four candy sticks to 3½" long. Glue one candy stick into each reindeer hole with brown icing, making sure they dry straight.

28. When the reindeer are dry, ice

the rest of the baseboard about ⅜" deep. Begin with the reindeer that stand closest to the sleigh (#7 and #8). Put a dab of icing into the hole in the center of reindeer #7. Insert the free end of the candy stick from reindeer #8 into the hole, and carefully stand them as a pair in the icing on the baseboard. Hold them steady

Sugar work

SAILBOAT

SOLDIERS

Santa's Sleigh Front

CUT 1 FROM RED DOUGH

ICING DESIGN

SANTA'S ARM
CUT 2 OPPOSITE OF
RED DOUGH ¼"THICK

Santa's Sleigh Sides

CUT 2 OPPOSITES OF RED DOUGH

SLEIGH - SLATS FOR CURVES   CUT 12 OF RED DOUGH

```
┌─────────────────────────────────────┐
│                                       │
│                                       │
│                                       │
│                                       │
│                                       │
│          Santa's Sleigh               │
│     Under-Carriage Platform           │
│                                       │
│        CUT 1  OF BLACK DOUGH          │
│                                       │
│                                       │
│                                       │
│              FRONT                    │
└─────────────────────────────────────┘

┌─────────────────────────────────────┐
│          Santa's Sleigh               │
│        Toy Shelf  Braces              │
│                                       │
│             CUT 2                     │
│                                       │
└─────────────────────────────────────┘

┌─────────────────────────────────────┐
│                                       │
│          Santa's Sleigh               │
│             Bottom                    │
│                                       │
│        CUT 1 OF RED DOUGH             │
│                                       │
│                                       │
│                                       │
│              FRONT                    │
└─────────────────────────────────────┘
```

for a minute. If they have trouble standing up, lean the front one in just slightly. When these reindeer seem to stand in place, repeat the process with the next two (#5 and #6), standing them with about 1" of space between the nose of one and the tail of the next. Continue with the last two pair. The reindeer are *very fragile* at this point, so do not bump or move the baseboard at all until the icing is completely dry.

29. For harnesses, roll green dough ⅛" thick and cut eight strips of dough ⅝" wide by 4" long. Roll red dough very thin and cut eight strips ⅜" wide by 4" long. Wet your finger with a drop of water and run it down the center of a green dough strip. Place a red strip centered over the green one. Repeat for all eight strips. With icing, attach one harness to each reindeer's middle, covering the candy stick hole. Wrap it all the way around.

30. Cut red licorice laces to size so they drape nicely between each reindeer. Use icing to attach the ends of the licorice from harness to harness. The last pair should drape into the sleigh. (Straight pins can be used to hold it in place while drying. When removing the pins twist them to loosen then pull them out.) Cover the ends of the licorice on each harness with icing, using a #18 star tip, and decorate with holly leaf sugar sequins and red nonpareil berries.

31. Attach silver dragée jingle bells to each harness with icing.

SLEIGH FRONT & BACK UNDER BRACE
CUT 2 OF BLACK DOUGH

SLEIGH CENTER UNDER BRACE
CUT 1   BLACK DOUGH

TAPE TO BACK HALF HERE

Santa's Sleigh
Runners

TAPE THE TWO HALVES TOGETHER AT DOTTED
LINE, THEN CUT 2 (OPPOSITES) OF BLACK DOUGH.

TAPE TO FRONT HALF HERE

Santa's Sleigh
Seat Front

CUT 1

Santa's Sleigh
Interior Seat Brace

CUT 1

Santa's Sleigh
Seat

CUT 1

Santa's Sleigh
Toy Shelf

CUT 1

Santa's Sleigh
Back

CUT 1 OF RED DOUGH

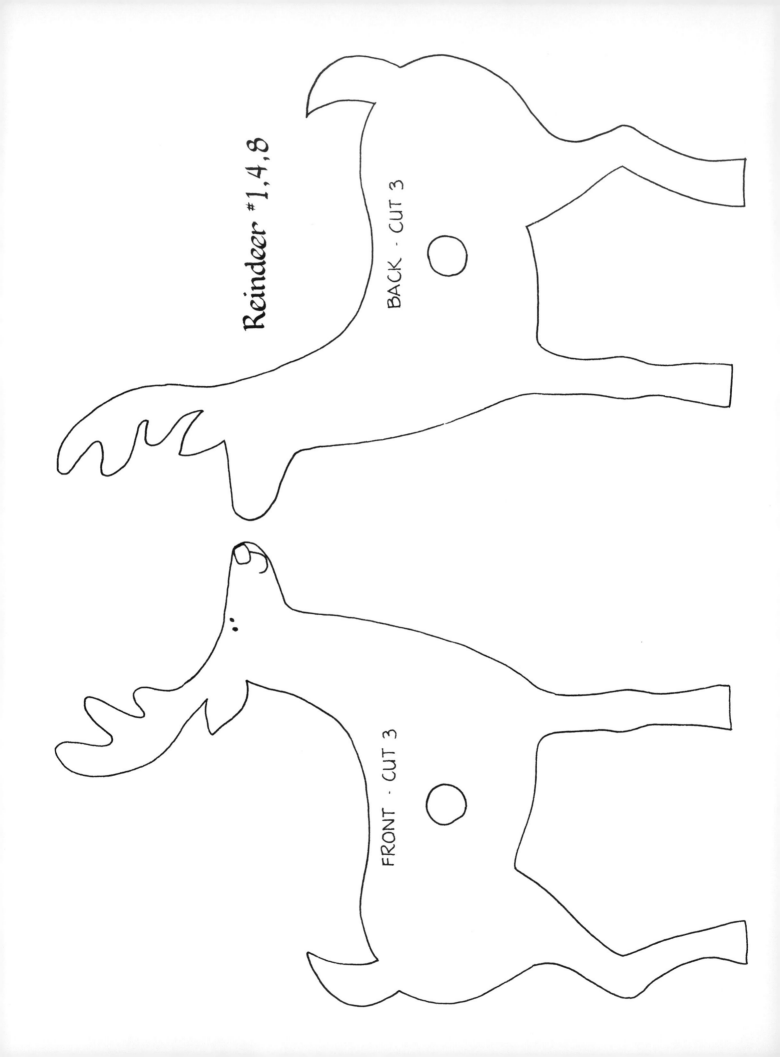

Reindeer #1,4,8

BACK - CUT 3

FRONT - CUT 3

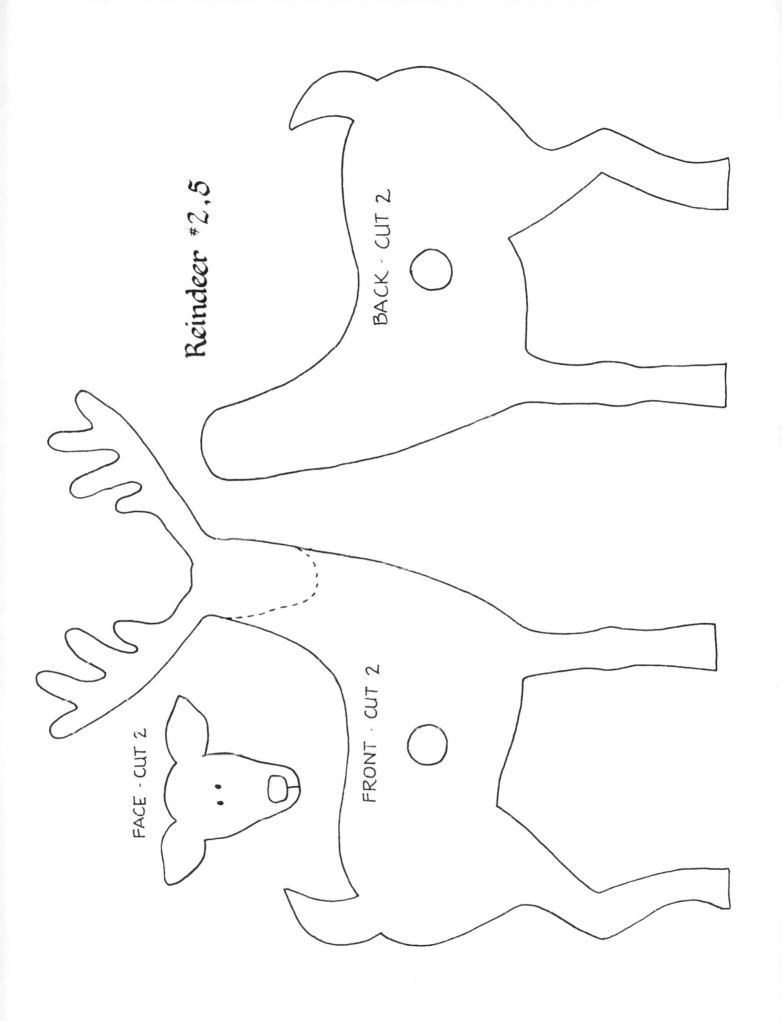

Reindeer #2,5

BACK - CUT 2

FACE - CUT 2

FRONT - CUT 2

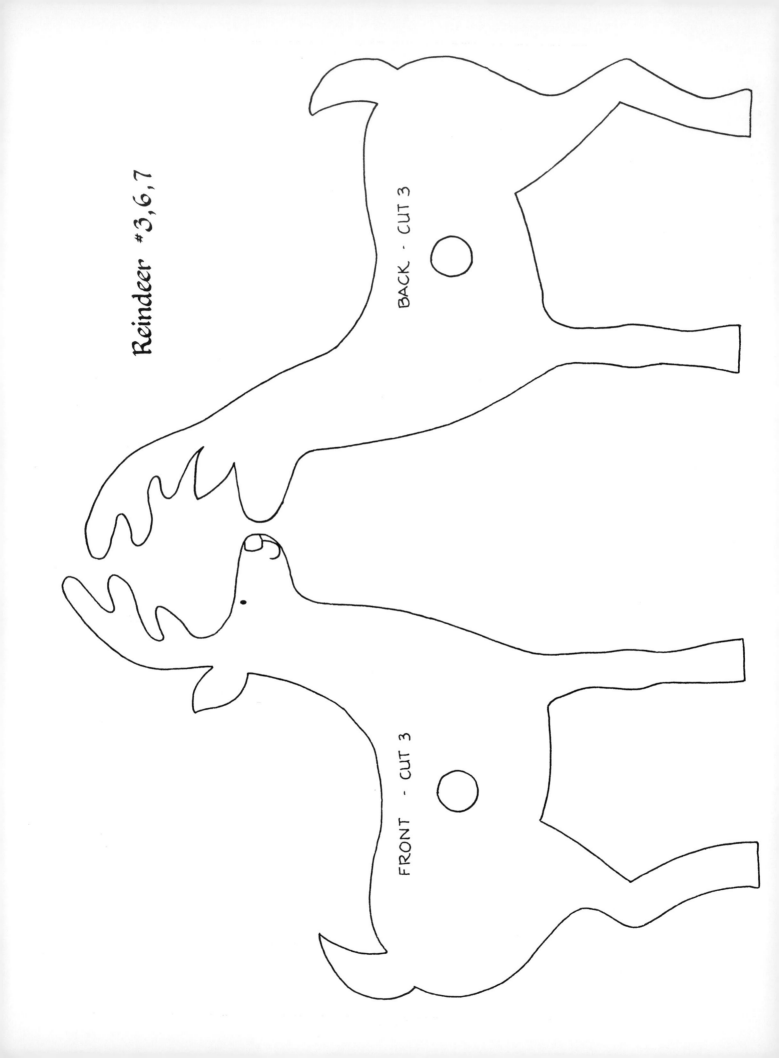

Reindeer #3,6,7

BACK - CUT 3

FRONT - CUT 3

CHRISTMAS BAKERY

1. Lay out and mark landscaping features and support dowel positions on the plywood board according to layout diagram. Use a ½" drill bit to drill holes for lampposts. Use a ⅜" drill bit to drill holes for tree placement and signposts. Use a ¼" drill bit to drill holes for support dowels.

2. Cover the board with the paper of your choice according to general instructions (page 9). Run your fingers over the surface of the board to find the drilled holes. Poke a finger or pencil into the holes to break the paper.

3. Prepare dough. Color brick red if you plan to make a brick building.

4. Make a night-light assembly (page 13) and attach it to the board if desired.

5. Roll the dough ¼" thick on non stick baking parchment. Cut the walls and score in brick lines according to instructions for brickwork (page 14). When cutting roof pieces, roll dough ⅛" thick. Cut and bake the following pieces:

CHRISTMAS BAKERY

Front and back - (front with windows and door, back with lamp cord notch).

Left side - 1

Right side - 1

Addition front and back - 2 (front with windows, back without)

Addition side - 1

Main roof - 2

Addition roof - 2

Front window shelf - 4

MATERIALS

plywood board 15 x 22 x ½"
paper to cover the board
tape
night-light assembly (page 13)
4 ¼" dowels 9" long
1 recipe gingerbread dough
½ recipe green dough
3–4 recipes royal icing
white chocolate clay (page 9)
silver dragée
chocolate bar
Christmas tree sugar sequins
red nonpareils
colored nonpareils
caramels
Necco® wafers (shingles and
   walkway)
2 candy sticks (lampposts)
yellow Starburst® candies
paste food colors: pink, green,
   red, brown, black
2 yellow Jumbo Jelly candles
spearmint leaf jelly candies

6. Roll green dough ¼" thick. Using nested 8-point star cutters, cut and bake five to six of each size and ten tree-top triangles.

7. Prepare the brick walls with icing mortar according to brickwork instructions (page 14). Do small areas at a time, as the icing dries quickly.

8. Pipe window and door frames using a #4 tip or a #47 tip for wider lines.

9. Pipe dentil trim across upper edge of wall using the smooth side of a #47 tip.

10. Pipe decorations over upper windows using a #1 tip.

11. Pipe white clapboards on addition walls with a #47 tip, if desired. Trim icing edges around windows with a sharp knife after icing has set about 15 minutes. Let dry.

12. Sink the dowels into the holes along building front.

13. Assemble the house walls on the board according to general instructions. Ice the dowels and attach the front wall to them as well. Before the roof is attached, build shelves inside the front windows. Make two rows of caramels, the back shelf being a bit higher than the front. Set front window shelves in place on caramels to make flat surfaces to show off "baked" goodies.

14. Make three gingerbread houses for the right front window by cutting caramels into house shapes. Add gum pieces cut to size, slices of jelly candy, or icing with sprinkles for a roof. Pipe tiny outlines and decorations with a #1s tip, and add colored nonpareils and jimmies for decoration. Let dry, then set the houses in the right front window on the shelves.

15. Plate of doughnuts: roll a small piece of white chocolate clay flat and cut a ¾" circle to use for a plate. Roll about eight tiny balls of gingerbread dough, flatten each slightly, and poke a hole in the centers with a skewer. Bake about 10 minutes to harden. Set cooled doughnuts on the plate with icing. Place in left front window.

16. Christmas cake: use a ¾" round canape cutter to cut two circles from a chocolate bar. Use white icing to stick the circles together. Ice the top with white and decorate with sugar sequin trees and red nonpareils. Let dry. Place in left front window.

17. Tray of cookies: roll a small piece of white chocolate clay flat and cut a ⅝" square for a tray. Use icing to stick red and green flower-shaped sugar sequins to the tray as cookies. Make two and place one on each window shelf.

18. Wedding cake: Roll a piece of white chocolate clay about ½" thick. Cut three circles sized 1⅛", ⅞", and ⅝" from the clay. Smooth the edges

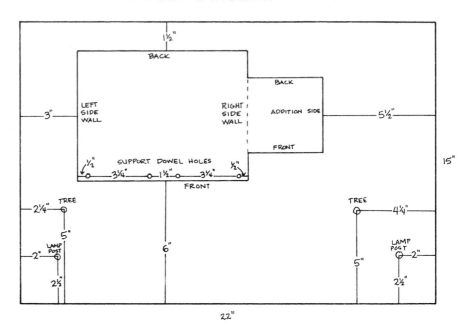

and stack the layers from largest to smallest. Decorate the cake with white icing swags, tiny pink and green dot flowers and leaves. Let dry. Place in left front window.

19. Make two lampposts according to general instructions (page 19). Let dry.

20. Attach roof according to general instructions (page 11) and shingle with Necco wafers.

21. Pipe #14 or #18 star beads over all seams.

22. Make sugar work roof decorations and sign decorations according to general instructions (page 16). Let dry.

23. Make awning pieces according to flood work instructions (page 16). After awning pieces are dry, assemble awnings separately from build-

ing. Let dry.

24. Pipe the lettering and edging on the sign using a #1 tip. Let dry.

25. Pipe the white base for the "Open" sign about ¾" long using the smooth side of a #47 tip. (Make several so you can choose the best one.) Let dry. Then, using black icing and a #1s tip, pipe the word "Open" on several of the bases. Let dry, then choose the best one and attach it to the door with icing.

26. Make garlands under windows and a wreath, if desired, according to general instructions (page 17).

27. Attach a silver dragée with icing for a doorknob.

28. Carefully attach the roof sugar work decorations with icing.

29. Carefully attach the assembled awnings over the front windows.

You may need to prop them up with a pretzel box or soup can while they dry. Let dry.

30. Build the stacked cookie trees according to directions (page 14).

31. Pave the walkway using broken black, brown, and purple Necco wafers or the paving material of your choice according to general instructions (page 18).

32. Ice the board about ¼" deep. Set the lampposts into the drilled holes and set the shrubs as desired. Set the sign in the front using the sign triangles as an easel back. Carefully place the sugar work sign decoration along the top of the sign with icing.

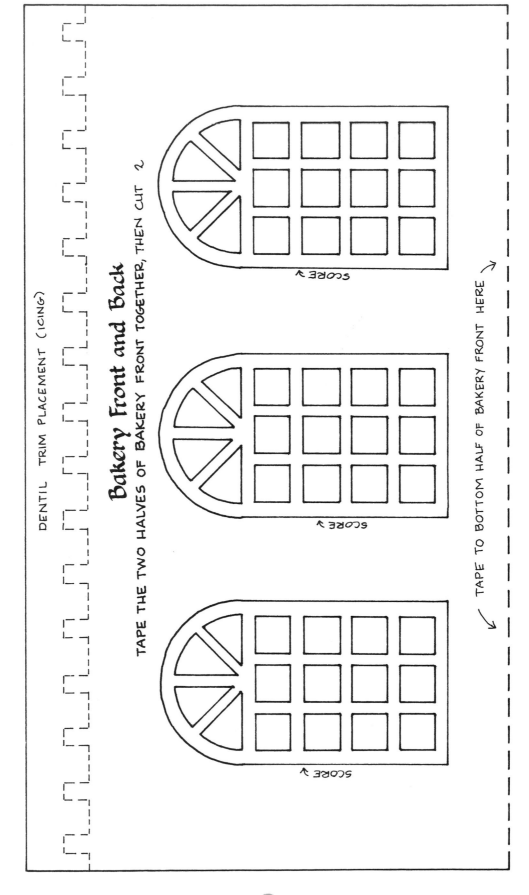

DENTIL TRIM PLACEMENT (ICING)

Bakery Front and Back

TAPE THE TWO HALVES OF BAKERY FRONT TOGETHER, THEN CUT 2

SCORE ↑

SCORE ↑

SCORE ↑

← TAPE TO BOTTOM HALF OF BAKERY FRONT HERE →

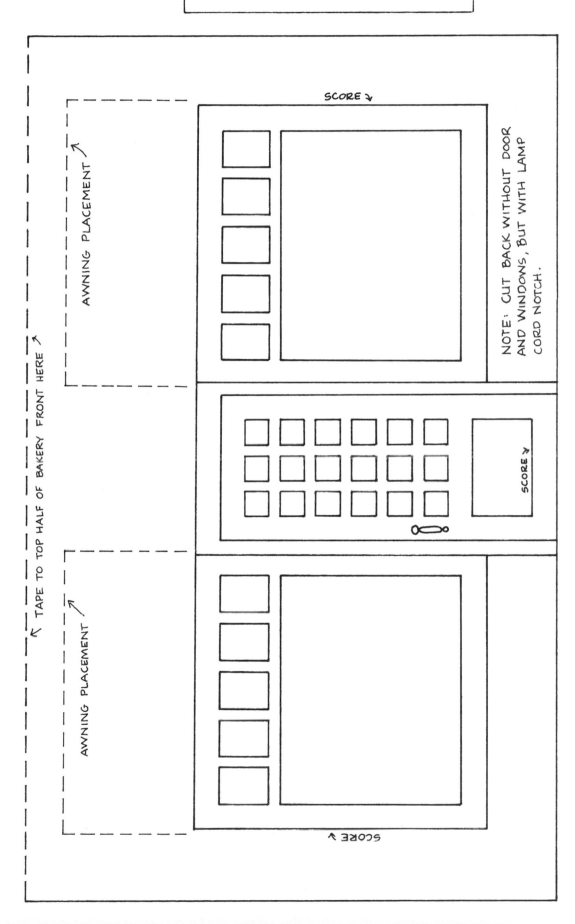

FRONT WINDOW SHELF

CUT 4

Bakery Front and Back

TAPE THE TWO HALVES OF BAKERY FRONT TOGETHER AND THEN CUT 2

← TAPE TO TOP HALF OF BAKERY FRONT HERE ↗

AWNING PLACEMENT ↗

AWNING PLACEMENT ↗

SCORE ↓

SCORE ↓

SCORE ↓

NOTE: CUT BACK WITHOUT DOOR AND WINDOWS, BUT WITH LAMP CORD NOTCH.

SCORE ↓

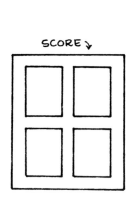

Bakery
Top Section of both Left and Right
Side Walls

↙ TAPE TO BOTTOM SECTION OF EACH SIDE WALL HERE ↘

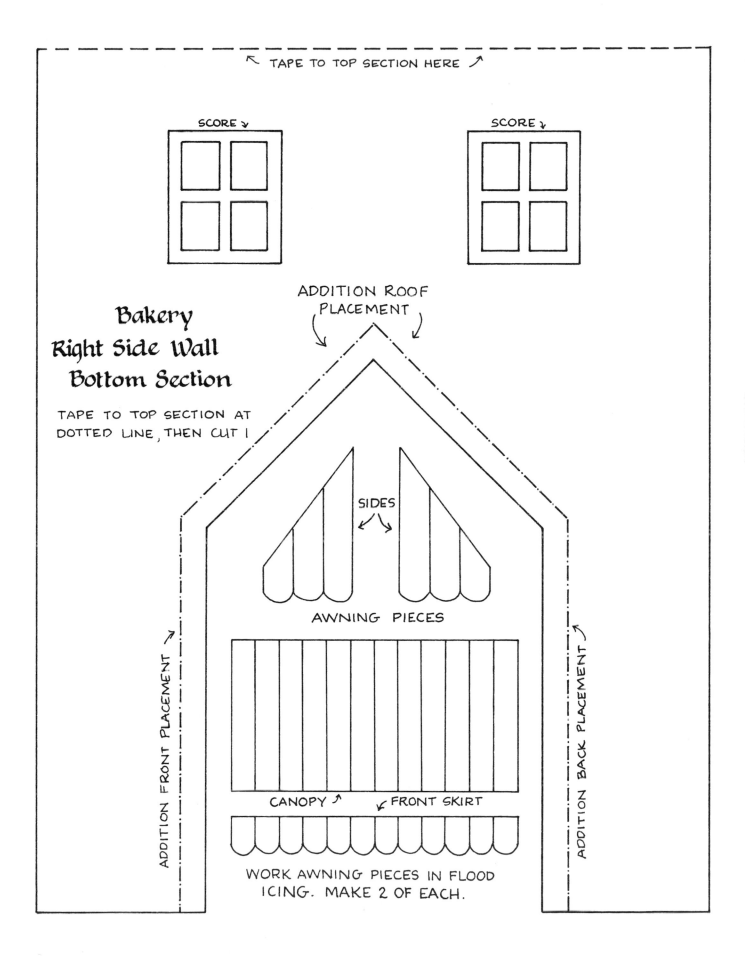

TAPE TO TOP SECTION HERE

SCORE ↓

SCORE ↓

Bakery
Right Side Wall
Bottom Section

TAPE TO TOP SECTION AT
DOTTED LINE, THEN CUT 1

ADDITION ROOF
PLACEMENT

SIDES

AWNING PIECES

ADDITION FRONT PLACEMENT

ADDITION BACK PLACEMENT

CANOPY ↗   ↖ FRONT SKIRT

WORK AWNING PIECES IN FLOOD
ICING. MAKE 2 OF EACH.

↖ TAPE TO TOP SECTION HERE ↗

SCORE ↘

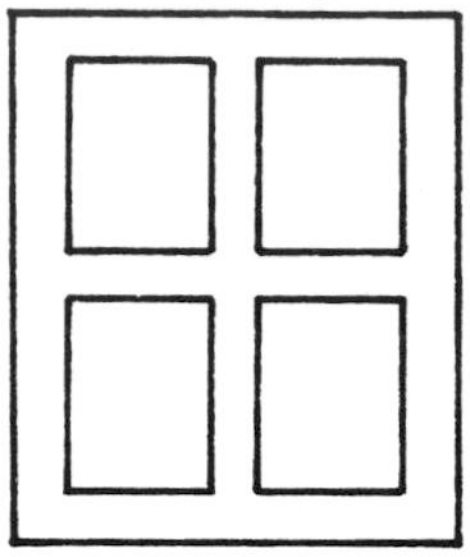

SCORE ↘

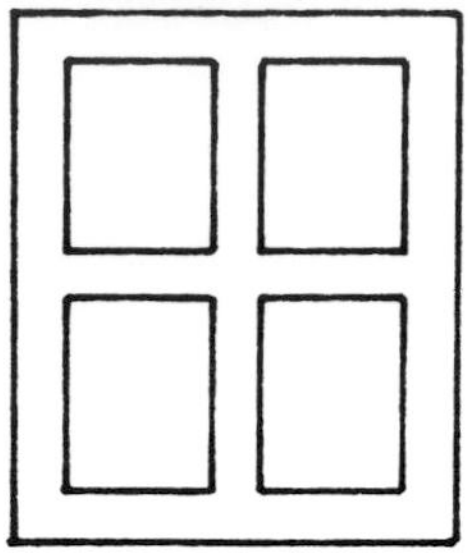

Bakery
Left Side Wall, Bottom Section

TAPE TO TOP SECTION AT DOTTED LINE, THEN CUT 1

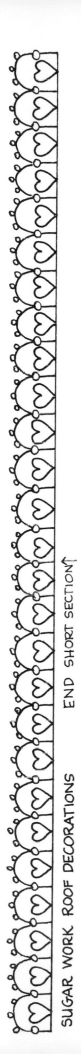

SUGAR WORK ROOF DECORATIONS   END SHORT SECTION↑

Bakery Main Roof

CUT 2

SUGAR WORK SIGN DECORATION

SIGN
EASEL BACK
CUT 2

SIGN - CUT 1

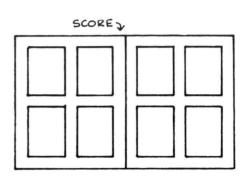

SCORE↓

Bakery Addition
Front and Back

CUT FRONT WITH WINDOWS
CUT BACK WITHOUT

SCORE↓

Bakery Addition Side

CUT 1

Bakery Addition Roof
CUT 2

GEPPETTO'S TOY SHOP

1. Lay out and mark landscaping features on the plywood board using the diagram provided. Drill holes for fence posts, lamppost, and tree with a drill bit to match the diameter of your candy canes.

2. Cover the board with your choice of paper according to the general instructions (page 9) and prepare dough (page 8).

3. Roll the dough to a ⅛" thickness. Cut and bake the following pieces:

GEPPETTO'S TOY SHOP

Front - 1 (with windows)

Back - 1 (without windows)

Bow window - 1 (baked on a 3" diameter can set in a cradle of aluminum foil)

Bow window ceiling and sill - 2

Bow roof side sections - 2 (opposites)

Bow roof center sections - 2

Left side wall - 1

Right side front and back walls - 2

Right side wall - 1

Right front and back walls - 2 (front with windows, back without)

Right side roof, front and back - 2 (opposites)

Shutters - 6

Roof peak - 2

Roof slats - 10

Roof brackets - 10

4. Roll brick-colored dough ¼" thick

MATERIALS

- plywood board 15 x 15 x ½"
- paper to cover the board
- tape
- night-light assembly
- 1 recipe gingerbread dough
- ½ recipe green dough
- 2 recipes royal icing
- Wheat Chex® cereal
- paste food colors: red, black, green, orange
- sliced almonds
- green sugar sequins for garland
- red nonpareils
- Starburst Fruit Chews®
- small red-hot candies
- spearmint leaf jelly candies
- emery board
- gum balls (large and small)
- candy canes or sticks
- toothpicks
- chocolate jimmies
- Crows® black gum drops
- 1 jumbo jelly candy (lamppost light)
- small colored ball candies (for "Toys" sign)
- 1 banana Runts® candy
- assorted hard candies

and cut and bake the following pieces:

Chimney - 1

Chimney front and back - 2

Chimney sides - 2

Chimney top - 1

5. Roll green dough ¼" thick. For the large tree, use nested 8-point star cutters. Cut and bake three each of the six sizes, five tree-top triangles, and six half tree shapes for the smaller tree. See Trees in general instructions (page 14).

6. Make one recipe of royal icing.

7. Make a snowman (page 17).

8. Make toys as follows:

A. Jack-in-the-Box

Cut one each of red, orange, and yellow Starburst fruit chews in half to make two thin layers of each color. Stack the layers back up: red, orange, yellow, orange, red. Press together firmly, but keep the square shape. Stick the last yellow layer on the upper back edge for a lid.

For Jack: Cut a slice (⅛" thick) from a spearmint leaf jelly candy. Cut notches into the edges of the slice. Place the slice on top of the box—this will be Jack's collar. Use a gum ball for his head. Use tiny bits of pink Starburst for his cheeks. Place his head on the sticky green collar. Pipe his eyes and mouth with black icing and a #1s tip. Then glue on a tiny red ball candy with icing for his nose. Pipe a circle of icing on his head and place half of a Runts banana candy for his hat and tiny red ball candy for a pom-pom. Set aside to dry. Note: If icing is not sticking well to gum balls (for faces), use an emery board to file off the shiny surface.

B. Train: Cut Starburst fruit chews into train engine and the train car shapes, each one a different color. Glue on tiny red-hot wheels with icing. Let dry. Decorate as desired.

C. Pinocchio (by front door): Place the following on baking parchment: for head, roll a small ball of dough and flatten it slightly to ⅝" diameter. Insert a ⅝" piece of toothpick for his nose and place two round sugar sequins for cheeks. For his body, roll a small egg shape and flatten slightly to ⅝" wide by 1" long. Place under the head so they just touch. Roll two pieces of dough to ¼" wide by 1" long. Place on parchment touching body for legs. For arms, roll two pieces ¼" wide by 1" long. Do not attach. Flatten a tiny part of the arm for the hand and make a small cut on each hand to be the thumb. Make a knife blade indentation at each elbow and knee. Bake 12 to 15 minutes. Make icing colors and prepare parchment icing bags with red, green, and black icing. Pipe white eye dots and place green nonpareil eyes. Pipe smile in black. Pipe white socks at ankles. Let dry. Pipe sleeves on arms and shirt on body with red icing. Place green nonpareil buttons. Let dry. When red icing on body is dry, pipe green suspenders, short pants, and hat. Make a feather

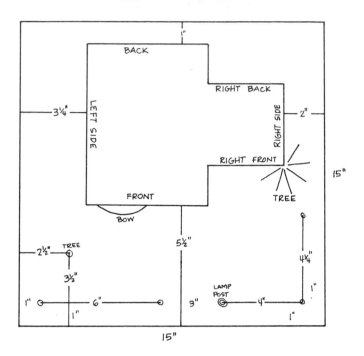

for his hat with a tiny slice of red licorice. Let dry. Lay him on nonstick parchment and pipe black shoes and attach his arms with red icing. Let dry overnight. Turn over and pipe his back—shirt, suspenders, and hat. Let dry.

D. Presents: Pipe bows on candies (hard candies, Starbursts, striped round peppermints all work well). Let dry.

E. Make sugar work soldiers and sailboat using patterns given and following general instructions (page 16).

9. Pipe the white base for the "Open" sign about ¾" long using a #47 ribbon tip smooth side up. (Make several so you can choose the best one.) Let dry.

10. Make a lamppost according to general instructions (page 19).

11. Make picket fence sections according to general instructions (page 19). You will need one section 5¾" long and two sections 3¾" long. Cut fence posts to size: you will need four posts 2½" long.

12. Prepare chimney pieces with "mortar" as in general instructions (page 14).

13. Pipe "Geppetto's" and the little top star on the front wall with a #1 or #1s tip. Pipe "Toys" with a #2 tip. Place small round candy balls on the letters as in the photo. With a #2 tip pipe the heart-and-dot design over the front door. Let dry.

14. At the top of the bow window piece, attach bow window ceiling to inside curve with icing. At the bottom of the bow window piece, attach bow window sill to inside curve with icing. Let dry.

15. With front wall lying flat, glue bow window in place with icing. Then attach the bow window roof pieces with icing. Begin with the two side roof sections, then place the center sections. Let dry.

16. Pipe the hinges, door handle, and "Open" sign string using a #1 tip and black icing. With a #1s tip, pipe the word "Open" on the dry white bases made earlier. (Again, make several so you can choose the best one.) Let dry.

17. Make and attach night-light assembly to board as per instructions (page 13).

18. Assemble toy shop walls as per general instructions (page 9), being very careful to support front wall with the bow window. With icing, set sugar work soldiers and sailboat in the bow window on a stack of caramel candies.

19. The roof on the toy shop is different from any other roof in this book. Because of the slight curve, the main part of the roof must be made with slats. Begin by gluing the roof brackets in place with icing at the top edges of the left side wall and right side front and back walls according to the pattern pieces. Next, attach roof peak pieces to main roof peak with a #6 tip. Then attach roof slats to wall edges and to each other (see below). Each side will use five slats. On the right side of the roof use whole slats until you get to the roof brackets, where you will need to cut the piece to fit, one for the front and one for the back.

20. Attach right side roof, front and back. Let set.

21. Attach chimney to right side wall at chimney markings and pipe a decorative bead with a #14 star tip on each side of chimney.

22. Build chimney top on right side roof.

23. Shingle the roof with Wheat

Chex cereal or the roofing material of your choice according to general directions (page 11).

24. Shingle the bow window roof with sliced almonds.

25. Make garlands on windows and wreath on door as per general instructions (page 17).

26. Attach "Open" sign to door just under the string you piped earlier.

27. Pipe small red hearts on shutters and attach shutters to window sides with icing as indicated on

the pattern pieces.

28. Pipe decorative beading on roof edges and seams as desired. Pipe icicles on horizontal roof edges as described in general instructions (page 16).

29. Ice board about ¼" deep. "Shovel" the walk by pushing the icing to each side and sprinkle with crushed chocolate jimmies.

30. Build stacked cookie tree in left front corner according to general instructions (page 14). Top with a

star cut from a flattened Starburst.

31. Sink fence posts and lamppost into predrilled holes. Set fence sections in place with icing.

32. Place snowman, jack-in-the-box, large and small gum balls for balls, train, presents, spearmint leaf shrubs.

33. Build six-piece tree near right side of front.

34. Attach Pinocchio to wall near front door with icing.

35. Glue red gum balls to fence post tops with icing.

Geppetto's Toy Shop
Roof Peak
CUT 2

CUT 10

Geppetto's Toy Shop   Roof Slats

BOW ROOF
CENTER SECTIONS
CUT 2

BOW ROOF
SIDE SECTIONS
CUT 2
OPPOSITES

THIS EDGE TO WALL

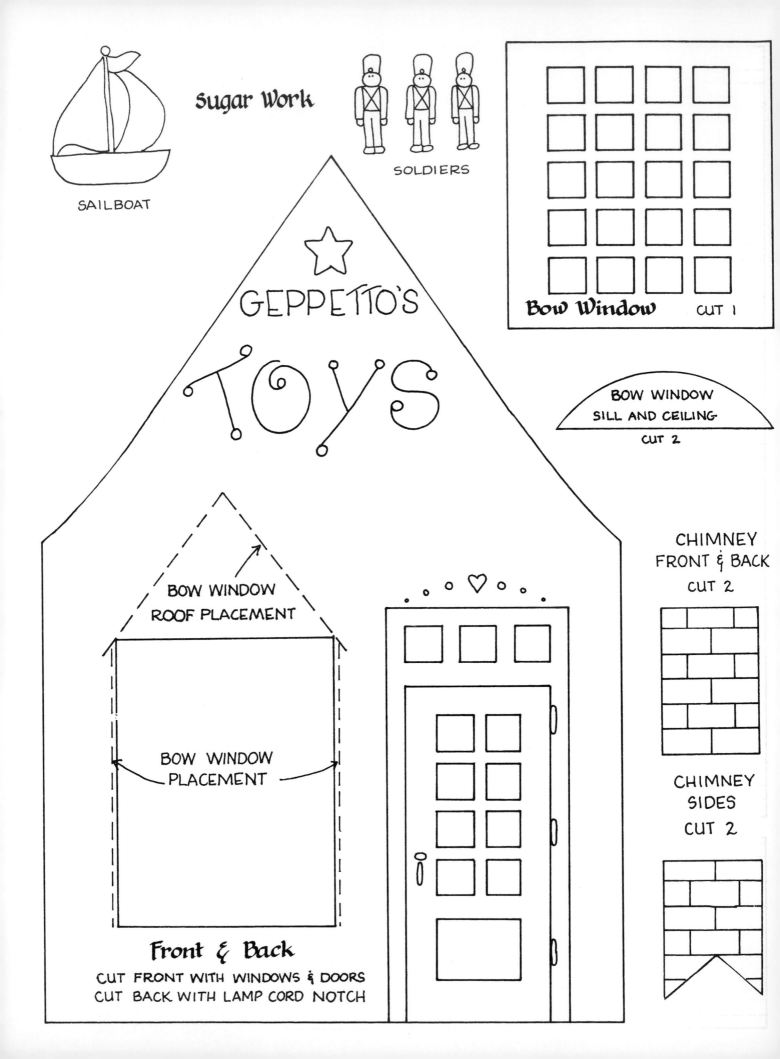

SAILBOAT

Sugar Work

SOLDIERS

Bow Window   CUT 1

BOW WINDOW
SILL AND CEILING
CUT 2

GEPPETTO'S
TOYS

CHIMNEY
FRONT & BACK
CUT 2

BOW WINDOW
ROOF PLACEMENT

BOW WINDOW
PLACEMENT

CHIMNEY
SIDES
CUT 2

Front & Back

CUT FRONT WITH WINDOWS & DOORS
CUT BACK WITH LAMP CORD NOTCH

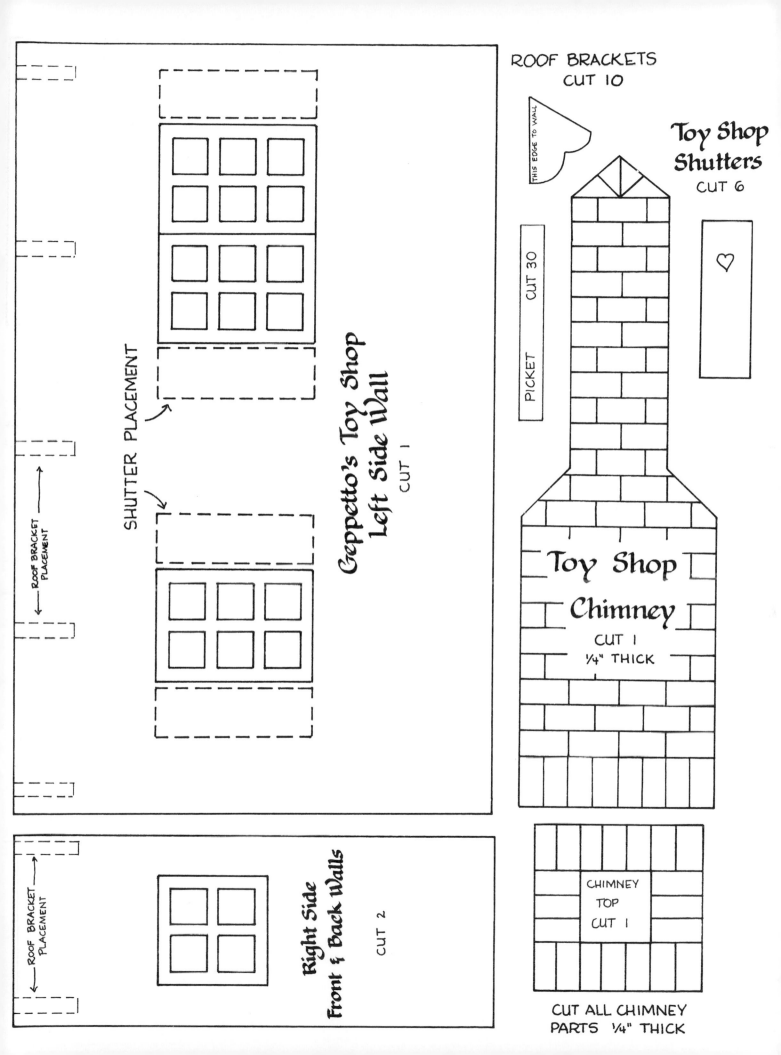

ROOF BRACKETS
CUT 10

THIS EDGE TO WALL

Toy Shop
Shutters
CUT 6

PICKET   CUT 30

SHUTTER PLACEMENT

ROOF BRACKET PLACEMENT

Geppetto's Toy Shop
Left Side Wall
CUT 1

Toy Shop

Chimney
CUT 1
¼" THICK

Right Side
Front & Back Walls
CUT 2

ROOF BRACKET PLACEMENT

CHIMNEY
TOP
CUT 1

CUT ALL CHIMNEY
PARTS ¼" THICK

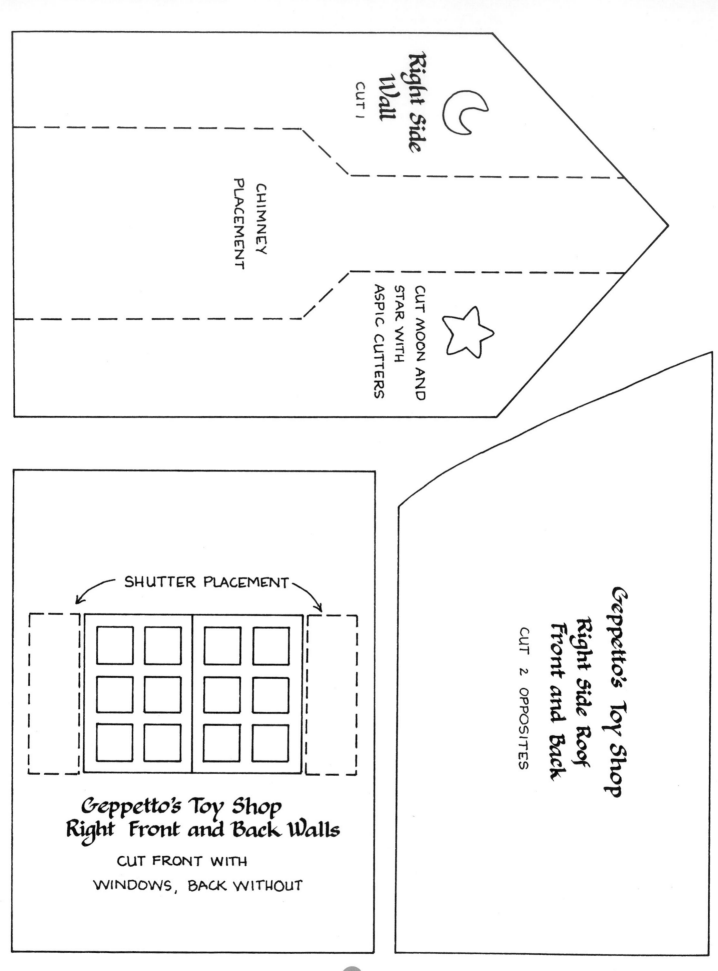

Right Side Wall

CUT 1

CHIMNEY PLACEMENT

CUT MOON AND STAR WITH ASPIC CUTTERS

Geppetto's Toy Shop
Right Side Roof
Front and Back

CUT 2 OPPOSITES

SHUTTER PLACEMENT

Geppetto's Toy Shop
Right Front and Back Walls

CUT FRONT WITH
WINDOWS, BACK WITHOUT

LANTERNS

Lantern Wall

1. Make the gingerbread dough and chill and make icing (page 8).

2. Cover the plywood board with the paper of your choice and secure with tape.

3. Roll the dough to a ⅛" thickness and cut four lantern wall panels of your choice. Cut four roof panels and one ring handle. Bake as directed.

MATERIALS

1 recipe gingerbread dough
1 recipe royal icing
plywood board 9 x 9 x ½"
paper to cover the board
tape
aspic cutters

4. Using a #18 star tip, assemble the lantern walls as you would a basic house (see general instructions, page 9). Let set about 30 minutes. Install a votive candle in a candle holder. Glue the candle holder to the baseboard with icing.

5. If the icing on the seams is too bulky or uneven for your taste, trim

Lantern Wall
CUT SQUARES WITH A ⅜" WINDOW CUTTER

it off with a sharp knife and repipe the seams with a star tip.

6. The lantern's roof is a "hip roof" i.e., all roof panels are placed so as to angle inward to a central point. It may help to have an extra pair of hands for this step. Pipe star beads on the upper wall edges and on the two angle side edges of one roof sec-

tion. Set the roof section into the icing on one wall section. Add the second and third roof sections and attach them to the lantern walls and first roof section. Pipe the last roof section and set it in place. Let dry. Note this is a more difficult roof, but patience will win over gravity.

7. Attach the ring "handle" if desired

with icing, and let dry. Repipe any beading that needs to be evened out.

8. Light the candle through the holes in the walls with extra long fireplace matches. **Note:** If you plan to keep your lantern lit for more than an hour or so, you may want to leave the ring handle off, as it gets a bit overdone by the heat of the candle flame.

Lantern Roof

CUT SHAPES RANDOMLY
WITH ASPIC CUTTERS

Lantern Wall

Lantern Wall

ORNAMENTS

Snowflakes

SNOWFLAKE ORNAMENTS

Prepare dough and icing (page 8). Roll dough about ⅛" thick on non-stick baking parchment. Using patterns cut from heavy paper, cut around outlines of designs. Using aspic cutters, window cutters, and regular drinking straws, cut designs into each cookie. Begin your design at the center of the cookie and work

outward. Follow the patterns or make up your own; there are as many possibilities as there are

snowflakes. Bake as directed in recipe. When cool, use the flood work technique (page 16) to cover the cookie tops with icing. It is nice to do both sides if you plan to hang them on a tree. When the flood icing is dry, use white icing and a #1 tip to pipe outlines, dots, and curls on the smooth icing surface. Let dry. Hang with ribbons.

ORNAMENTS

Hanukkah Ornaments

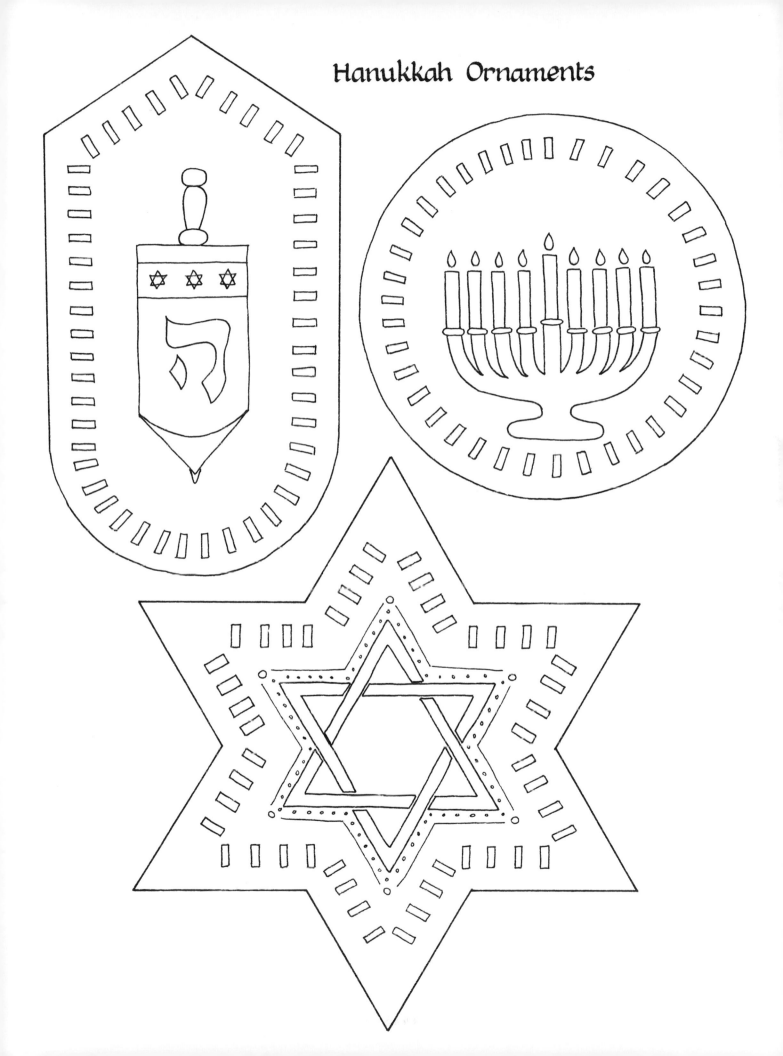

HANUKKAH ORNAMENTS

1. Prepare dough and icing (page 8). Roll dough ⅛" thick on nonstick baking parchment. Using patterns cut from heavy paper, cut around outlines of designs. Using a ⅛ x ¼" window cutter (see source list), cut holes for ribbon weaving around edges of designs according to pattern. Bake until golden brown. When cool, weave ribbons through holes around edges (silk ribbons work well) and tie off in bows at the top.

2. Using the flood work technique (page 16), pipe and flood designs on cookies. When flood icing is dry, you can highlight parts of the designs with luster dust. Mix a tiny bit of luster dust with a drop of orange or lemon extract and paint on with a soft paintbrush. Let dry.

GOLDEN CELTIC KEY ORNAMENTS

Prepare dough (see page 8). Using the piped gingerbread technique (page 14), pipe the key designs. Bake as directed or until golden brown. When cool, use a soft paintbrush to paint on gold luster dust mixed into orange or lemon extract. Let dry.

Golden Celtic Keys

ACKNOWLEDGMENTS

The concept of this book came from my heart because I love to do this kind of work, but the creation of it came because so many wonderful people helped in so many ways. From the bottom of my heart I would like to thank: Lydia Alfano, mother of four boys, who still found time to help with baking and building, always with a smile and without whom this book would never have come close to its deadline; Rita Brenenstuhl of the Confectionery House, who so generously shared ideas and products for this book; Wendy Pender-Cudlip for typing miles in minutes; Randy O'Rourke for taking such beautiful photographs and for making my work look so good; Delores Hetzko for her kindness; Cathy Yanik for the use of her dining room and for always calling to make sure I was still on the planet; Renate Tryon for her support and encouragement and who keeps bringing her friends to my classes; Juliana and Amanda for letting me use their wonderful toys; Ellen Prindle for friendship and being there in all kinds of weather; Gretchen Mastrogiannis, who accepts any mission set before her, even when she's on vacation; Richard Palan, who is always on the other end of the phone with support and an occasional dose of reality; Sue Katz and Naomi Warner for encouraging this opportunity; Ellen Cohen for being the calm in the storm; Dirk Luykx and Amanda Wilson for overseeing the design of this book; Karyn Gerhard for her disk and typing input; Gayle and Richard Meissner and their wonderful shop Recherché for supplying us with exquisite pieces and for letting us move in for the night; CK Products and Kencraft for generously supplying products to try; Bill and Elaine for helping out in every way they could; my mom and dad, who encouraged creating with the beans, not just counting them; my husband Kenny and my daughter Karen for all their love and patience; and all the people who liked my first book so much that it made this one possible. —T.L.

SOURCES

Primrose Cottage
8 White Oak Lane
Warren, CT 06754
(860) 868-0764
Window cookie cutters, nested 8-point star cutters, clear plastic rulers, gingerbread tool kits, aspic cutters, luster dust.

The Confectionery House
975 Hoosick Road
Troy, NY 12180
(518) 279-3179
Sheet gelatin, food coloring pens, nonstick baking parchment, CK products including gum paste, luster dust, sugar sequins, liquid and paste food colors.

CK Products
Ft. Wayne, IN 46808
(219) 484-2517
Luster dust, all kinds of sugar sequins, food colors, pastry bags and tips, cookie cutters, pans, etc. Wholesale only—ask for CK products at a local cake decorating shop.

Country Kitchen
3225 Wells Street
Fort Wayne, IN 46808
(219) 482-4835; 1-800-497-3927;
fax (219) 483-4091
Cake and candy-making supplies and CK products.

New York Cake
56 West 22nd Street
New York, NY 10010
(212) 675-CAKE
Cake and candy-making supplies.

Creative House Int'l.
102 South Richmond Street
P.O. Box 17
Fleetwood, PA 19522
(610) 944-8510; 1-800-346-4584;
fax 1-800-245-9511
All kinds of cookie cutters. Wholesale only—call for a local retailer.

Sweet Celebrations
P.O. Box 39426
Edina, MN 55439
1-800-328-6722;
fax (612) 943-1688
Baking and candy-making supplies.

Kencraft, Inc.
P.O. Box 1129
Alpine, UT 84004
1-800-377-4368
Candy sticks in all colors, gum ball buddies. Wholesale only—call for a local retailer.

Wilton Enterprises
2240 West 75th Street
Woodridge, IL 60517
(630) 963-7100; 1-800-772-7111;
fax (630) 963-7196
Pastry bags and tips, cake decorating supplies.

Recherché Studio
166 New Milford Turnpike
New Preston, CT 06777
(860) 868-0281
Fine antiques.